Inspired & Inspiring

Labs, Studios and Workshops for Creative Minds

The Deutsche Nationalbibliothek lists this publication in the
Deutsche Nationalbibliografie; detailed bibliographic data are
available on the Internet at http://dnb.dnb.de

ISBN 978-3-03768-235-7
© 2018 by Braun Publishing AG
www.braun-publishing.ch

1st edition 2018

Project coordination: Editorial Office van Uffelen
Editor: Susanne Bauer, Julia Heinemann, Johanna Schneider
English translation: Judith Vonberg, London
Graphic concept: Studio LZ, Stuttgart; Agnes Essig, Lisa Zech
Reproduction: Bild1Druck GmbH, Berlin

Inspired & Inspiring

Markus Sebastian Braun

Labs, Studios and Workshops for Creative Minds

BRAUN

Content

Where art thou, Muse [...]?

…wrote William Shakespeare in the opening line of *Sonnet 100*, lamenting the absence of inspiration. Poets tend to blame the daughters of Zeus and the goddess of memory Mnemosyne when they lack creative ideas. In his poem *The Theogony*, written around 700 BC, Hesiod listed nine muses: Calliope (who presides over epic poetry), Clio (history), Euterpe (music, song and lyric poetry), Erato (love poetry), Melpomene (tragedy), Polyhymnia (hymns), Terpsichore (dance), Thalia (comedy), and Urania (astronomy) are responsible in the world of Greek mythology for generating "artistic" ideas, but it is also their job to sing the glory of their father's victory over the primordial gods. They live their lives in allegiance to the god Apollo—who presides over music, poetry and song and who is, in a way, their overseer—by the Castalian Spring at the foot of Mount Parnassus, whose waters give the gift of poetry.

For the less "artistic" arts, the muses are only indirectly responsible. For example, Clio, charged with historiography, is also duty-bound to stimulate painters of historical works—the most prestigious genre in the visual arts. So it is no coincidence that the model reproduced by the artist painted by Jan Vermeer can be read both as Clio and as a personification of the art of painting.

In the Middle Ages, as to be expected for pagan figures, the Muses were out of work, but still left their mark in the terms "music" and, later, "museum." Their place was taken by "divine inspiration," which also had an ancient role model. In *In De Natura Deorum*, written

↑ Jan Vermeer
The Art of Painting, 1665–1668
Oil on canvas, 130 cm × 110 cm
Kunsthistorisches Museum, Vienna

in 45 BC, Cicero describes the afflatus (divine inspiration) as an unexpected breath of wind that captures poets. It is this wind that also gives sound to the Aeolian harp—Aeolus is the god of the winds.

Whether it's airborne inspiration or a dutiful, personified muse, the exact prerequisites for a brilliant idea are still largely unknown. In-depth and long-term study of a subject certainly helps and this is exactly what "creative professionals" do. In addition to perseverance, inner independence, non-conformism and self-confidence all play decisive roles in the creation of something new. And, solely in the case of artists, slipping into a manic-depressive state also seems to be something of an advantage, as the psychologist Kay Redfield Jamison found in a clinical study.

But a manic depression isn't necessary if one wants to become a better artist. So we return to the muses. It was in the Renaissance that the nine women finally found employment once more, enlightening artists or researchers and scholars, or encouraging them to engage in persistent but not narrow-minded confrontation with their respective subjects. In the following centuries, the nine Greek sisters were increasingly replaced by highly specialized personal muses. Charlotte Freifrau von Stein for Johann Wolfgang von Goethe, Camille Claudel for Auguste Rodin, Yoko Ono for John Lennon, Dora Maar for Pablo Picasso, and Maude Gonne for William Butler Yeats—to name just a few. But muses needn't be life-long—many are temporary. For Salvador Dalí, both his wife Gala and the singer Amanda Lear functioned as muses, and Lou Andreas-Salomé was not only the muse of Friedrich Nietzsche, but also Rainer Maria Rilke and Sigmund Freud. Alma Margaretha Maria Schindler stylized herself into a muse for, among others, Gustav Mahler, Walter Gropius, Franz Werfel and Oskar Kokoschka, intensifying the femme fatale aspect of her personality, which has always been part of the muse's role.

Many of the muses mentioned here were themselves creative people, so of course it can be assumed that the partners served as sources of inspiration for each other. Nevertheless, it is usually only the female partner—following on from the mythological sisters—who is titled as "muse." But of course there are also male muses, for example Baptiste Giabiconi and Brad Kroenig for Karl Lagerfeld.

But can rooms replace the muses or the afflatus? They certainly can, as this volume shows, and in many different ways. It is often objects or relationships and scenarios involving them that can stimulate fresh perspectives on an issue or generate new ideas entirely. The design of a room can therefore make a decisive contribution to inspiring an artist. Space can also be integrated into a building as an unused canvas—emptiness waiting for the creation of something new. These spaces can invite both mental absorption and fallow time, can generate complexity and demand new forms of spontaneity—all of which are factors that creativity research has found to be beneficial. And such spaces are, unlike the muses, never absent, unwilling or sick.

↗ Bertel Thorvaldsen
Euterpe, Muse of Music, c. 1836
Plaster, 64 cm diameter
Thorvaldsens Museum,
Copenhagen

Design Technology Block, St James School
Ashford, England

Architects → Squire and Partners
Location → Church Road,
Ashford TW15 3DZ, England
GFA → 175 sqm
Completion → 2016
Client → St James School
Inspired & inspiring → product design
Main materials → timber
www.squireandpartners.com

Occupying an area within the St James School grounds, previously home to an ad hoc collection of sheds and storage units, the new Design Technology Block was designed to accommodate students and teaching staff as well as an office, plant and store room. Taking inspiration from the craftsmanship and simple technology of timber-frame buildings in the southeast of England, the building envelope is clad in a black vertical weatherboard and cover strip system, within which a concealed gutter and flush pyramidal roof light ensure the purity of the building form is not compromised. The dark external cladding provides a striking contrast to the light Douglas fir timber interior. Passive ventilation was achieved via electrically operated vents in the roof apex. An added benefit of using timber was the natural absorption of sound, aiding acoustic attenuation. Inside, traditional pegged mortise and tenon joints within the timber frame are counterpoised by steel hex-head fixings and sheets of birch-faced ply panels lining the walls. Exposing this timber structure and employing traditional construction methods were an important part of the project, displaying to the students the beauty, longevity and practicality of timber as a building material, and providing a simple and practical backdrop for the workshop activities within. The architect's approach to the new block was to combine historically referenced construction with modern technology, inspiring the students and serving the school for years to come.

→ 20 students and two
teaching staff find space in
the new building.

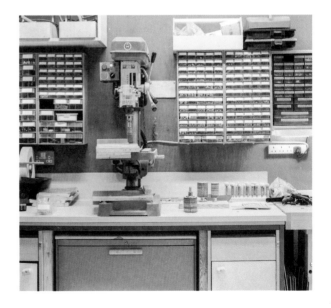

← Ground floor plan of the
Design Technology Block.

↖ The Douglas fir is visually
characterized by a tight grain
and minimal knots and is
recognized for its strength.

↑↑ The students can use
all sorts of tools.

↑ Design and technology
merge in one place.

Visible Studio
Bath, England

Architects → Invisible Studio
Location → The Rocks, Ashwicke,
Bath SN14 8AW, England
GFA → 55 sqm
Completion → 2014
Client → Invisible Studio
Inspired & inspiring → architecture
Main materials → timber
www.invisiblestudio.org

This new studio was built by the practice with the help of neighbors and friends using untreated and unseasoned timber grown in the woodland that surrounds the structure. The studio stretches on two floors and comprises a 55-square-meter enclosed space accessed via a bridge from the slope and an open workshop below where employees can build full-scale models. No one who worked on the project had any experience in construction. The project was an exercise in establishing a system of building that could be constructed by unskilled labor, with minimal drawings, allowing ad hoc discoveries and improvisation, and avoiding the tyranny of predetermined design. The "mistakes" of the unskilled team remain evident in the building, and no attempt was made to conceal them. A mobile saw was rented for two days and all of the timber used was milled in that time. This informed the building design, which embraces the constraints of minimal cost and design. For example, the cladding that was milled at the end of the two days was just enough to partially clad the studio. The project was scaffolded with timber that was ultimately used for the bridge and floor, negating the need for expensive scaffold hire. The windows were scavenged from a skip, and the floor paint was left over from an earlier project. All of the boarding used is the cheapest possible grade, and the insulation is carefully pieced together from off-cuts. The structure is heated by waste wood from the woodland, and water from the roof feeds into an attenuation pond that forms a natural habitat.

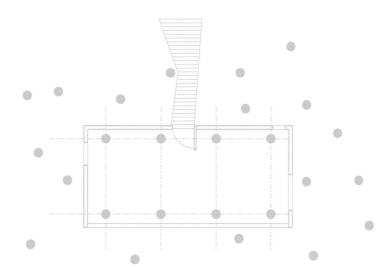

↑↑ The studio of the architects lies in the middle of the forest.

↑ Ground floor plan with the surrounding trees.

← The building has two floors and is reached via a bridge.

↑↑ Since the studio was made from its surrounding trees, it adapts perfectly to the forest.

↑ The footings were mixed by hand, and designed to be the most minimal possible.

↑↑ Since the house stands on stilts, even a car can be parked under it.

Agentur Jung von Matt / Neckar
Stuttgart, Germany

Architects → Bottega + Ehrhardt Architekten
Location → Neckarstraße 155,
70190 Stuttgart, Germany
GFA → 2,000 sqm
Completion → 2011
Client → Jung von Matt / Neckar
Inspired & inspiring → advertising
Main materials → warm gray rubber,
birch multiplex panels, felt
www.be-arch.com

The creation of new offices for the advertising agency Jung von Matt / Neckar involved the conversion of two stories of a former job center in Stuttgart with a total floor space of 2,000 square meters. While preserving the existing framework of the building, the architects modernized the old office cubicles and created new office areas with glass partitions. The distinctive Solnhofen flagstones were kept, as were the old wooden doors, to which glass panels were added to improve the flow of light through the interior. Generous staircases connect the two floors and serve as a central forum, where events, presentations, rest breaks and meetings can take place. Warm gray rubber flooring is used throughout the interior, enhancing the aesthetic sense of harmony between the stories. The central forum is enclosed by walls made of birch multiplex sheets that feature the firm's logo—a stylized Trojan horse. Behind these are the directors' offices and a large conference room. The entrance area and a second conference room are located opposite the two main staircases. A series of wooden cubicles are integrated into the central part of the building. Designed with both seating and standing options, these spaces feature natural felt on the interior and offer employees a place of cozy and quiet retreat. A cafeteria on the lower level contains a long wooden table and benches. This unique project is characterized by the combination of the old building structure and the new spatial interventions, generating a new and exciting working environment for Jung von Matt/Neckar.

↑ The wooden think tanks interlock with a folded glass partition wall to the offices.

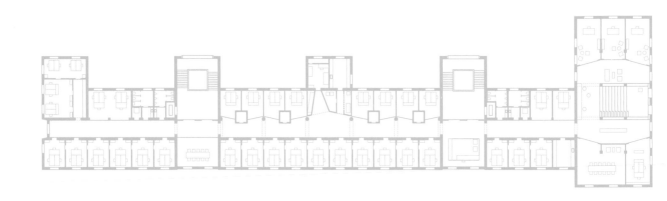

↖ Ground floor plan of the advertising agency.

↖ In the central forum, the weekly Monday round with news from the agency takes place for all 150 employees.

↑↑ Attached to the forum, an open library supports inter-action in the office building.

↑ The firm's logo is a stylized Trojan horse.

Terra Cotta Studio
Điện Bàn, Vietnam

Architects → Tropical Space
Location → Điện Phương Ward,
Điện Bàn District, Quang Nam, Vietnam
GFA → 98 sqm
Completion → 2016
Client → Le Duc Ha
Inspired & inspiring → art
Main materials → clay solid brick,
solid wood, concrete, bamboo
www.khonggiannhietdoi.com

This project is a cube-shaped building, each side measuring seven meters. Surrounding the studio is a bamboo frame platform used for drying out terra-cotta products and home to two large benches designed for relaxation. This raised platform also serves as a fence to separate the studio from the workshop area. The outermost layer of the studio is made with solid clay brick, evoking a traditional Vietnamese furnace. The studio also bears the characteristics of Champa culture as this area used to be part of Tra Kieu, the capital city of the Hindu Champa Kingdom, between the fourth and seventh centuries. Breezes and sounds from outside enter the interior through holes generated by the interweaving of the building's bricks. A three-story wood frame system on the interior generates a number of 60-square-centimeter modules, which integrate shelves for displaying artworks as well as a staircase, hallways and benches. The artist works on the ground floor, which is flooded with natural light from sunrise to twilight and is home to the turntable. Visitors can watch the artist at work from the mezzanine level. Flooding is a risk for the site, so high shelves were incorporated into the design, where both finished and unfinished works can be stored.

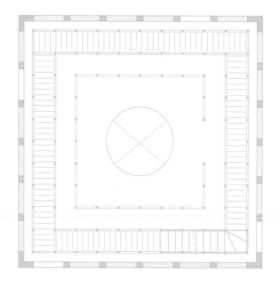

← The turntable to work is lit
by natural sunlight throughout
the day.

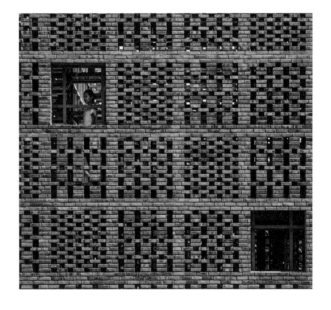

← Ground floor plan with the different wall structures.

↖ On the platform with bamboo frames, the terra-cotta products can be dried in the sun.

↑↑ The building has a cube shape, which is therefore completely symmetrical.

↑ The massive clay tiles around the building are reminiscent of a traditional Vietnamese stove.

Onder de Leidingstraat
Eindhoven, The Netherlands

Architects → MaSa (Marjan Sarab Architecture)
Location → Leidingstraat 45,
5617ZA, Eindhoven, The Netherlands
GFA → 163 sqm
Completion → 2014
Client → Nicole van Kempen, Dario D'Alessandro
Inspired & inspiring → food
Main materials → tiles, wood, steel, concrete, glass
www.marjansarab.com

Onder de Leidingstraat houses a range of functions: a café, restaurant, deli and supermarket with organic products. The clients' vision was a place where organic cooking is combined with a homemade style of food. The whole complex works not only as a restaurant but also as an educational platform. The kitchen has been placed in the center of plan, allowing customers to watch as their food is being prepared and establishing a separation from the supermarket area. Onder de Leidingstraat is located on the ground floor of Anton building, an old TV and Radio Philips factory building in Strijp-S Eindhoven. In the restaurant, different areas are designed based on different needs of consumers and workers: Along with a bar and supermarket, the consumer area houses a sunlit space incorporating high tables with cables for workers, low tables and chairs designed for eating, and armchairs and couches for lounging and reading. The raw industrial and modern design references the history of the building, which used to be a Philips factory. It was restored and transformed by diederendirrix architecten in 2013. The building now offers space for 130 lofts and commercial spaces such as shops and restaurants on the ground floor. The industrial character of the building has been restored by the careful preservation of most of the materials on the floors and walls. The rest of the space is kept white and simple while furniture and plants are used to add color to the space.

↑ A special feature of Onder de Leidingstraat is the raw design of the old factory.

↗ It is used as creative space for meetings.

↑↑ The products used
in the café and restaurant are
all organic.

↑ Visitors can not only eat in
the restaurant, but also watch
their meal being prepared.

↗ Ground floor plan of
the café, restaurant, deli and
supermarket.

→ Because of the lots of
glass and its large room Onder
de Leidingstraat is brightly lit.

Atelier Tenjinyama
Takasaki, Japan

Architects → Ikimono Architects
Location → 323-1 Kaizawa-machi,
Takasaki-si Gunma 370-0042, Japan
GFA → 62 sqm
Completion → 2011
Client → confidential
Inspired & inspiring → architecture
Main materials → concrete
sites.google.com/site/ikimonokenchiku

This atelier has a very primitive architectural form, designed to protect the interior from rain and wind. It was assembled from just four walls and a roof—and the design method was just as simple. The architect began by creating a box and installing a window to connect the life of the interior with the surrounding urban area. The ceiling is transparent to allow views of the often blue sky, while trees were planted inside the structure itself, bringing man-made and natural elements into dialogue with each other. Indeed, nature was a key factor in the design of the studio, which was created to enable enjoyment of the natural elements such as wind, rain and sunshine, rather than defending the inhabitants from them. The city of Takasaki in northern Japan experiences many thunderstorms during the summer and dry winds during the winter: this atelier offers the ideal location to appreciate these weather events.

↑ The open-plan studio
creates the feeling of standing
directly on the street.

↑↑ The studio unites office and workshop.

↑ The studio stands out with its clear stature and the large windows.

→ The brightness of the studio is perfect for a precise and creative work.

↗ The ground floor plan shows the working area inside the building.

↑ Many plants and an open
roof merge building and nature.

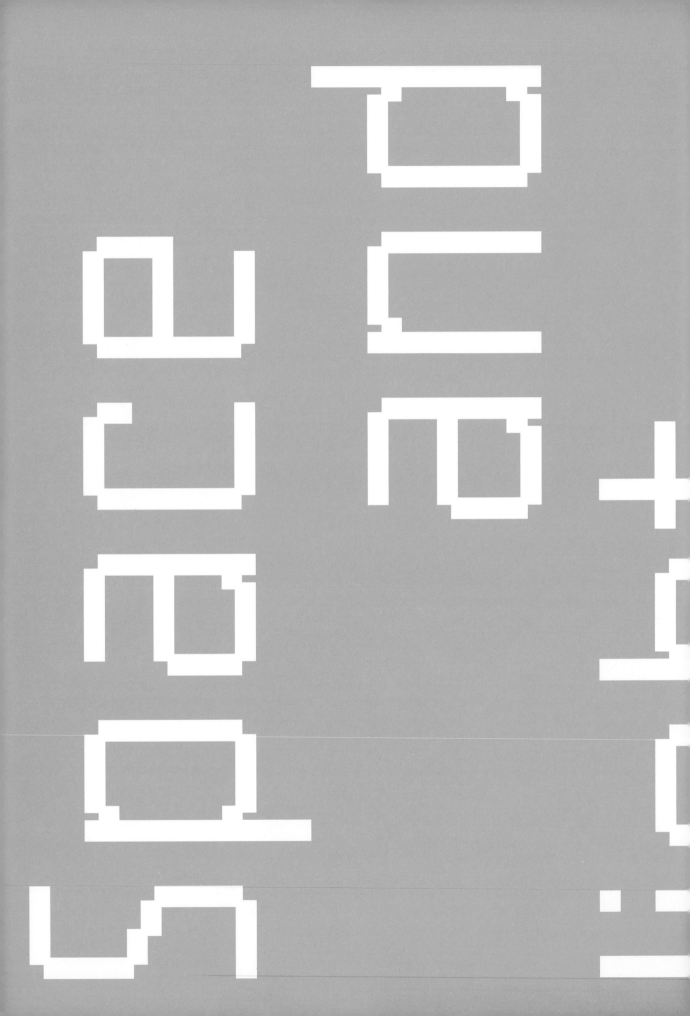

"Space and light and order. Those are the things that men need just as much as they need bread or a place to sleep."

→ Le Corbusier

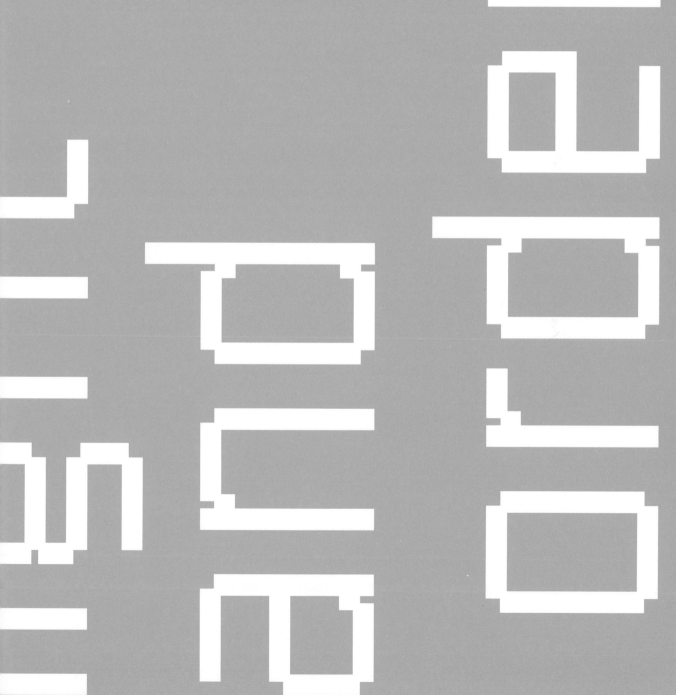

Studio Fuksas
Rome, Italy

Architects → Fuksas
Location → Piazza del Monte di Pietà, 30,
00186 Rome, Italy
GFA → 1,100 sqm
Completion → in progress
Client → Fuksas
Inspired & inspiring → architecture
Main materials → oak parquet, terra-cotta
tile floor, transparent and opaline glass,
grassello lime, wax, brushed natural iron
www.fuksas.com

The home of Italian architectural firm Fuksas in Piazza del Monte di Pietà, Rome, is situated in a Renaissance building, whose present configuration dates back to the second half of the 19th century. The atelier has four floors and hosts offices, design rooms, a model-making space and meeting rooms. A lift with an iron platform, crystal walls and steel fixtures connects the first floor with the Aquarium Room, where meetings take place. In some parts of the atelier, the lime putty treated walls have been renovated in order to bring out the plaster and paint layered by time. Hanging on the walls are several architectural models housed in display cases as well as paintings and sketches created by Fuksas. In Massimiliano Fuksas' personal room, a wide iron sliding door acts not only as background but also as support for sketches, images and pictures of various projects. The exposed ceiling is made of white painted wooden trusses. Close to the office building, in Via di S. Maria in Monticelli, an exhibition and deposit area houses the models for the firm's most important projects. A stairway links the three levels of the building, whose basement is home to some ruins of ancient Roman baths.

↑↑ The walls have been restored in order to emphasize the various layers of plaster and paint overlaid over time.

↑ Interior of the historical palace which hosts Studio Fuksas on four levels in Rome.

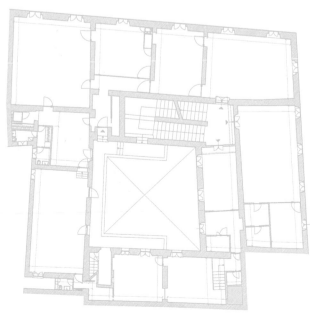

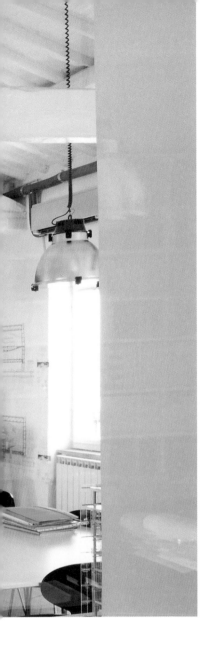

← Ground floor plan of the atelier.

↖ The large sliding partition wall in the background performs as a display for images and pictures of some projects.

↑↑ View of the work spaces with exposed ceilings and wooden trusses painted in white.

↑ In the foreground, a model of "New headquarters of Regione Piemonte" in Turin, Italy.

Rustic Canyon Art Studio
Santa Monica, CA, USA

Architects → FINNE Architects
GFA → 85 sqm
Completion → 2008
Client → confidential
Inspired & inspiring → art
Main materials → redwood exterior siding,
zinc roofing, Douglas fir windows, structural
steel columns and beams, concrete floors
www.FINNE.com

The Rustic Canyon Art Studio occupies a thin, triangular sliver of property close to the Pacific Ocean in Santa Monica, California. Connected to the main residence by both a footbridge and an automobile bridge, the studio is a retreat designed for art and exercise. The triangular plan is delineated by the property line and a hillside to the east and the Rustic Canyon Creek Channel to the west. A simple steel column and beam system placed on the interior of the studio allows the roof plane to be lifted off the building. The building's columnar system corresponds to a subterranean system of large concrete caissons that extend nine to 12 meters below ground level. An art studio and exercise area are housed inside the building, with sliding glass panels creating a partial separation wall between the two areas. Continuous Douglas fir clerestory windows around the studio perimeter separate the walls from the roof plane. High windows bring soft, diffuse light into the building, creating optimal natural lighting for the art studio. The exterior walls are 30 to 35 centimeters thick to allow for horizontal air distribution. The roof is on an incline from south to north due to the triangular plan and is further cut on the diagonal and lifted to create large, north-facing clerestory windows for the studio. Sustainability was a key project goal from the beginning.

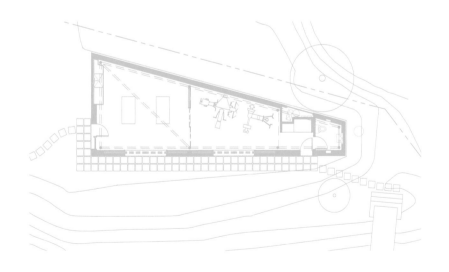

↑↑ The studio is surrounded
by nature—a hillside to the east
and the Rustic Canyon Creek
Channel to the west.

↑ The triangular floor plan
with art studio, exercise area
and mechanical room.

↑↑ Insulation values 60%
higher than conventional
construction were achieved
by using double 2x4 walls.

↑ High clerestory windows
provide extensive natural
light and ventilation throughout
the house.

→ Sliding glass partition
doors between art studio and
exercise area.

CHICHI Office
Osaka, Japan

Architects → koyori + atelier salt
GFA → 45 sqm
Completion → 2015
Client → CHICHI Graphic design firm
Inspired & inspiring → graphic design
Main materials → olive veneer, brass light sockets
www.koyori-n2.com

The goal of this project was to differentiate CHICHI Office from other office buildings in the area, which is characterized by the presence of a large number of design studios and offices. The café therefore became a primary space within the design, which was developed on the assumption that relaxing spaces encourage the flow of ideas. The space was to be a hothouse for creativity. Clear partitions between the workspace and the meeting room were avoided and shade-producing plants were introduced to soften the atmosphere. The lack of walls means both the meeting room and workspace can be used for a variety of functions, while the plants were chosen for their adaptability to the changing seasons and their rapid growth. Employees can therefore sense the changing time of day and season, enhancing their sensitivity to the world around them. A simple and timeless olive finish was selected for the furniture. A glass wall divides the main interior spaces from the entrance hall, allowing as much natural light as possible to flow into the work areas.

↑↑ Shelf and plants in the center softly divide between workspace and meeting room.　↑ View to workspace from glass entrance hall.

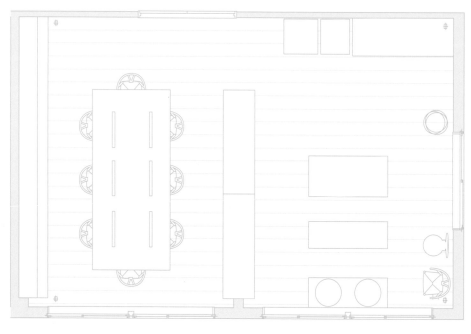

↑↑ Workspace surrounded by wood and light.

↑ Floor plan with the two work areas.

→ Both the meeting room and the workspace can be used differently.

↑ The many plants give the
office a cozy atmosphere.

Architect's Office
New Delhi, India

Architects → Spaces Architects@ka
Location → A21A, Basement, South Extension Part II,
New Delhi 110049, India
GFA → 140 sqm
Completion → 2013
Client → Spaces Architects@ka
Inspired & inspiring → architecture
Main materials → white oak, white paint,
cement texture paint
www.spacesarchitects-ka.com

This project involved the conversion of a 140-square-meter basement into an open office on two levels, the lower of which is used as a workstation. The goal was to generate a creative atmosphere where employees can enjoy their work. The main cabin with attached conference room is located at the rear to maintain privacy, while also remaining visually connected with the front office, home to a gallery with walls in cement finish. Open workstations connected by cantilevered wooden steps are found in the lower section, which is dominated by white in contrast to the upper space. A reception counter with a backlit glass panel and bookshelf displaying the firm's projects can also be found here. A green space with grass flooring and elliptical seating is used as a breakout zone. Two workstations for senior architects are located behind the seating area. The outer partition of the main cabin is inclined at both planes and designed in a fluid form with veneer cladding that continues onto the conference room ceiling, creating a visual transition. Ceilings are also used elsewhere in the design to create evocative effects, such as the multiple box panels on the ceiling near the reception and a hanging model inspired by the architects' thesis project. In the green area, the circular seating is reflected on the ceiling in an abstract pattern that continues into the rear space.

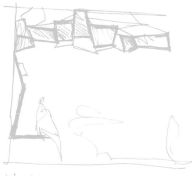

VIEW AT RECEPTION

CEILING AT RECEPTION

← Open workstations allow open cooperation between the employees.

↑ The ceilings are used in many different ways. In the front office, they also function as a gallery.

↗ Ground floor plan with the different areas.

→ The workstations, connected by wooden steps, are found in the lower section of the office.

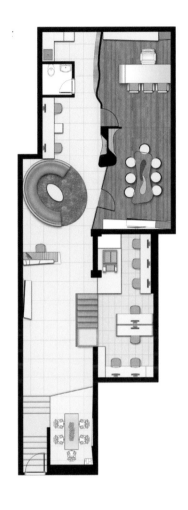

↑ The green seating area
invites for entertaining breaks.

Container Studio
Amagansett, NY, USA

Architects → MB Architecture
GFA → 90 sqm
Completion → 2008
Client → confidential
Inspired & inspiring → art
Main materials → steel, plywood
www.mbarchitecture.com

The client required an art studio close to her house, which was
renovated in 2008. She was looking for a simple structure providing
her with around 90 square meters of space that could be completed on a tight budget and would be both inviting and reflective. The
solution was to use two 40' high-cube containers—each of which
costs $2,500—perched over a nine-foot foundation wall / cellar.
By cutting 75 percent of the floor of the containers, the architects
were able to move the painting studio to a lower level via a wide
staircase and take advantage of a high ceiling. The staircase itself acts
as a transitional space for viewing artwork, while the upper floor
provides a more intimate work area and a sitting area. The containers
were painted dark charcoal to maintain continuity with the original
house and to recede into the shadows of the dense wooded site.

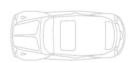

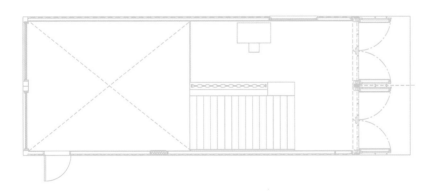

↑↑ The building is very simple, both from the outside and inside.

↑ The ground floor plan of the studio shows the large creative area.

← Although the building looks very dark from the outside, due to its color and the windows it is very bright inside.

↑ Through the large glass pane much light can shine during the day.

↑↑ A wide staircase leads down to the art studio.

↑ A small workplace is in the upper gallery.

Tree Top Studio
Adelaide, Australia

Architects → Max Pritchard Gunner Architects
GFA → 25 sqm
Completion → 2013
Client → Max Pritchard
Inspired & inspiring → architecture
Main materials → plywood sheeting, perspex windows
www.mpgarchitects.com

The architect required a small home studio on his tree-studded coastal site. The house, built 27 years ago, is an elevated steel-framed glass-sided structure, thirty meters long and four and a half meters wide, utilizing the efficiency of the structural system of a cable stayed bridge. Only four columns support the structure, causing minimal disturbance to the landscape. An entirely different approach was adopted for the studio, while still emphasizing the structure and minimizing the footprint. The circular tower appears as a crafted timber-clad cylinder, just four meters in diameter and rising over two levels. Entry to the top level is via a bridge, linking back to the sloping ground. The timber frame structure is expressed on the inside and outside, with hardwood battens aligning with the framing and covering the plywood joints. A dynamic cantilever roof plane is framed with radiating timber beams, again expressed with hardwood battens. The radiating pattern of roof and ceiling is repeated on the floor. Whilst the main house has the purity of a modernist structure of expressed steel framing, the studio adds a sense of decoration in the expression of structure. Believing that architects can gain valuable practical knowledge from the construction process, the architect built his own studio, including the design and construction of the central circular table.

↑ The furniture, bookshelves,
table and chairs also follow the
design of the roof and the walls.

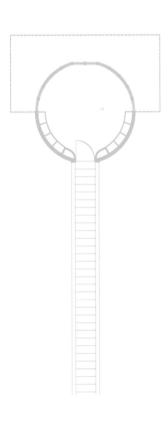

↑ The two-level circular tower is wrapped in golden plywood sheeting.

↑↑ The architect designed his own studio in the tree-studded coastal site of his property.

↗ Floor plan of the upper floor.

→ With its timber frame structure, the Tree Top Studio fits perfectly into its surroundings.

Kialatok
Paris, France

Architects → Septembre
Location → 74 Rue Philippe de Girard,
75018 Paris, France
GFA → 150 sqm
Completion → 2016
Client → Kevin Berkane, Florence Pellegrini
Inspired & inspiring → food
Main materials → pine plywood, concrete,
stainless steel, massive larch wood, resin epoxy
www.septembrearchitecture.com

Kialatok is a social enterprise offering world cooking classes by self-taught chefs from different cultures. Septembre designed their new space in the heart of the cosmopolitan area of Pajol, in Paris' 18th district. A suitable location was found in the bottom floor of a city block in mutation, well exposed to the street. The client wanted a flexible space that could be adapted depending on the format of the cooking class, while the design should reflect the diversity of different food cultures. The space is organized by a single large storage wall, where objects for each culinary culture used during the workshops are on display. This wall—visible from the street through large windows—generates the identity of the space by reflecting the universe of world cooking, and the diversity of different food cultures. Various types of utensils and dishes are displayed as well as the tools needed to experience a particular food culture, such as chopsticks and a porcelain spoon. The objects are both pedagogic instruments and aesthetic additions to the space. The materials selected for the space remain subtle, in order not to detract from the colorful objects on the storage wall. The walls and shelves are in pine plywood, and the tabletops and trestles are made of larch. Raw concrete on the ceiling and backdrop wall has been preserved. The light gray, polish resin floor reflects light and brightens the space. Stainless steel covers the central kitchen island.

↑↑ The cooking island in the middle of the room allows several people to work at the same time.

↑ Kialatok not only provides space for preparing meals, but also for eating them.

↑↑ Cooking utensils and ingredients from all over the world can be taken from the large shelf.

↑ On the shelf there are also tools to experience the different food cultures.

↗ Ground floor plan of Kialatok with space in use.

→ Pine plywood and raw concrete let the essentials stand in the room—cooking and learning together.

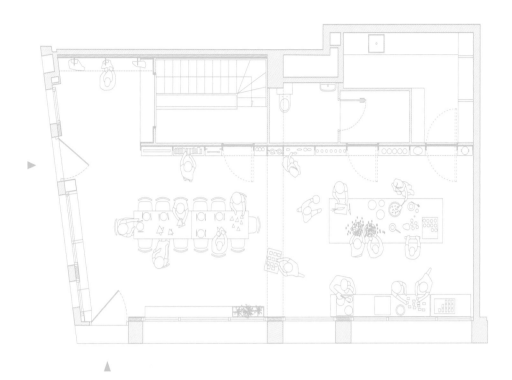

"I don't think that architecture
is only about shelter, is only
about a very simple enclosure.
It should be able to excite you,
to calm you, to make you think."

→ Zaha Hadid

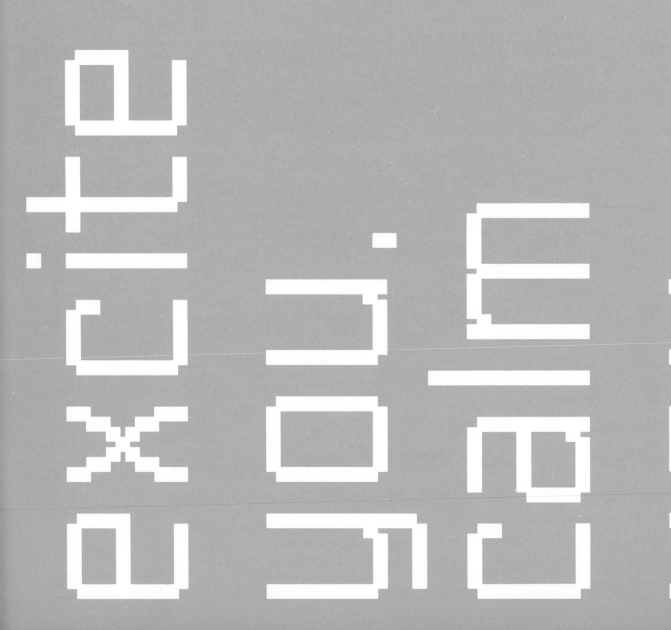

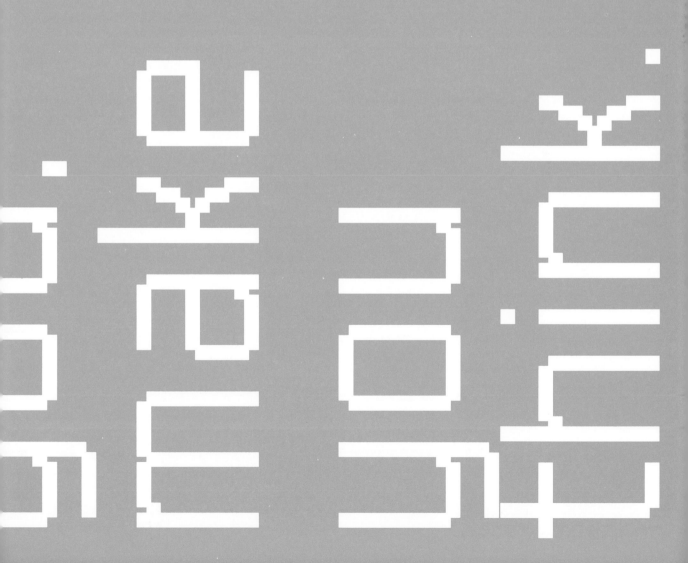

BAKE Sendai
Sendai, Japan

Architects → Yota Kakuda Design, In On Out
Location → Sendai Station, 1-1-1 Chuou Aoba-ku Sendai
Miyagi, 980-0021, Japan
GFA → 40 sqm
Completion → 2016
Client → Bake Cheese Tart
Inspired & inspiring → pastries
Main materials → cast aluminum tiles
www.yotakakuda.com

BAKE Sendai, located in Sendai, Japan, is a bakery that sells baked cheese tarts. The designer began by creating a series of gray cast aluminum tiles that would cover the entire interior space. Since he spends much of his time designing industrial products, it seemed natural for the designer to design the tiles—the key creative element in this project—himself. A yellow wall containing boxes stands in contrast to the rest of the space, while a transparent oven allows customers to see and learn about the baking process. By minimizing the design and the furnishings, the process of baking is allowed to take center stage. The industrial design elements generate the feeling of a factory, where visitors can view the various stages of the production process. The employees also benefit from the sparse design, which reduces distractions and enables greater creativity. According to the designer, the design of this space needs little explanation—and it's this simplicity that makes it so successful.

↑↑ The production of
cheese tarts is the center
in the minimalistically
designed room.

↑ The name in the cast
aluminum tiles is part of the
walls design.

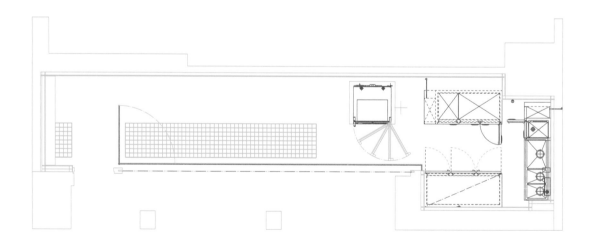

↑↑ The bakery is poorly decorated and the colors are monochrome—only the yellow wall stands out.

↑ Ground floor plan of the bakery.

→ The gray cast aluminum tiles cover the entire room and make it look almost clinical.

Scott & Scott Studio
Vancouver, Canada

Architects → Scott & Scott Architects
Location → 299 19th Avenue East,
Vancouver, BC V5V 1J3, Canada
GFA → 70 sqm
Completion → 2014
Client → Scott & Scott Architects
Inspired & inspiring → architecture
Main materials → Douglas fir
www.scottandscott.ca

A year after the launch of their practice, architects Susan and David Scott completed the refurbishment of the historic commercial space in their 1911 East Vancouver residence. Once a butcher's shop and a grocery store, the space has been stripped back to a simple volume lined with Douglas fir boards and completed with black stained fir plywood millwork. Using familiar materials from their region, the architects built the space themselves with a couple of carpenters. The fir was supplied from a sawyer on Vancouver Island with whom they have worked for several years. Three fir logs were selected, milled and cut to suit the width and height of the space. The work was completed in a manner rooted in traditional methodology while utilizing the availability of modern tooling. The unsalvageable south-facing storefront had been infilled by a previous owner and was restored to an area of glass consistent with the original size using a single high-performance unit. Informed by a desire to create work which is fundamental in its architecture and supportive of a variety of uses over time, the priorities were to maximize the use of natural light, enhance the connection to the neighborhood, use regional materials that have a known providence, and acknowledge the lumber-based building culture of the Pacific Northwest. The interior fir boards are finished with a variant of warm applied 19th-century bee's wax floor finish with the solvent replaced with Canadian Whiskey. The tables are hand-stitched finished leather tops on blackened galvanized steel bases.

↑ The main component of the construction is wood, which is displayed in this building very minimalistically.

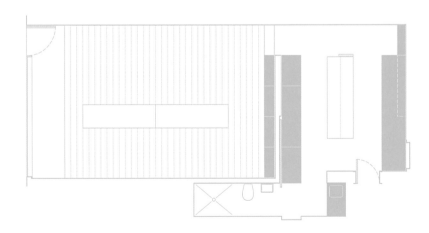

← Both planning and
construction—in the studio,
the models of the archi-
tectures are produced, too.

↑↑ The large glass front of
the studio also gives an insight
from the outside.

↑ The simple floor plan of
the studio.

↑↑ Due to their simplicity,
the rooms offer plenty of space
for creative work.

Atelier
Barcelona, Spain

Architects → Miriam Barrio Studio
Location → Santaló Street, Barcelona, Spain
GFA → 40 sqm
Completion → 2015
Client → confidential
Inspired & inspiring → art
Main materials → micro-concrete, steel, pine
www.miriambarrio.com

The challenge began with the reconversion of a small soccer field into an atelier—a place to unleash imagination and create art. The design proposal focused on the generation of an inspiring space, flooded with light via a fully glazed structure supported by a super light black steel carpentry frame. The ceiling and walls allow jets of light to enter the interior of the studio, while rolling screens can be used to mitigate overly strong sunlight. In the interior, a light-colored box of continuous micro-cement on the floor and walls allowed the architects to introduce colorful pieces without overpowering the vision of the whole. The industrial-style and recovered furniture combines mainly wood and iron, out of which the architects created completely customized pieces to meet the needs of an artist. These included mobile tables with space for storing and organizing boxes, brushes, and all kinds of knick-knacks. Some of the furniture was customized by the artist, such as doors that are now large collages. The terrace was finished in micro-cement, creating volumes that give rise to planters and orchards, benches and a large chill-out space.

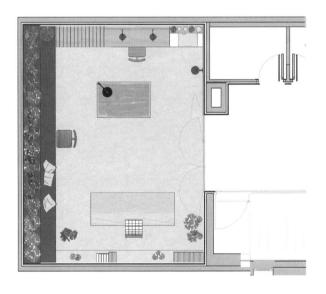

↑↑ Through the large
windows a lot of light
passes through and helps
to work creatively.

↑ Ground floor plan of the
atelier, a former soccer field.

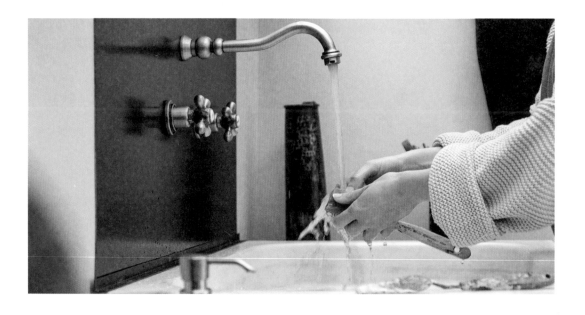

↑↑ Some sketches of
the artist.

↑ The combination of
industrial design and
recovered furniture makes
the atelier unique.

↑ The simple design of the building and the artistic atmosphere inside harmonize well.

Red Bull Studios
Berlin, Germany

Architects → Nau2, Optimist Design
GFA → 400 sqm
Completion → 2015
Client → Red Bull Germany
Inspired & inspiring → music
Main materials → steel and concrete frame with
acoustic linings and copper exterior cladding
www.nau2.com
www.optimistdesign.com

Optimist Design created a sculptural music studio for Red Bull's
addition in Berlin to their series of global music spaces. Built in
a disused power station from the 1920s, the new contemporary interiors contrast perfectly with the old. With Nau2 driving the design
locally, the project was conceived as combining two worlds—a social
space outside and a series of box spaces inside determined by geo-
metry, sound and technical requirements. A particular challenge
was to ensure the space met high technical and acoustic standards
while also looking good on camera. The new studio hosts recording
and mixing spaces and communal areas with multi-perspective views
into the recording rooms. The studio wanted to highlight the link
between the old power station roots and the Red Bull brand associa-
tion of power and energy. To achieve that, they clad the interior
walls with copper bands to add depth and to capture natural light
entering through the glass roof. A giant curved staircase flows cen-
trally through the space, surrounded by integrated furniture to create
seating areas around the steps that lead towards an abstract play-
ground and lounge area. Muted colors and warm materials delineate
a variety of spaces and niche areas. A hang-out lounge was crafted
on the upper level with views into the recording space. The architects
wanted the space to foster creativity and make people feel comfort-
able. Both the formal language as well as the choice of material
finishes and colors create a balanced visual effect while establishing
a dialogue between old and new.

↑↑ Artists, both established
and up-and-coming, are invited
to record in the studio.

↑ Inside the old power station,
a new sculptural volume was
added, with a landscape of
stairs and lounge areas around.

↑↑ The prismatic shape ensures optimal sound for the recording and mixing spaces.

↑ A dark graphite color was used to create a strong backdrop and striking contrast to the rest of the design.

→ Optimist Design wanted to ensure the space was very Berlin-specific by keeping the industrial feel to the interior.

↗ The exterior is clad with over 1 km of copper bands—a nod to the location's origins as a power station.

NOMA Lab
Copenhagen, Denmark

Architects → GXN
Location → Strandgade 93,
1401 Copenhagen, Denmark
GFA → 200 sqm
Completion → 2012
Client → NOMA
Inspired & inspiring → food
Main materials → Nordic wood
www.gxn.3xn.com

At the heart of the creation of NOMA Lab was the need for an inspiring experimentarium where chefs could improve their skills in developing Nordic cuisine. The commission was given to 3XN's Innovation Unit, GXN, whose experimental design suited NOMA's innovative gastronomy. The NOMA Lab, which is connected to NOMA, is located in a former warehouse that is listed on the national registry of protected buildings. The tight restrictions meant that GXN was required to design the interior without using so much as a single nail in the walls or flooring. The approach was to design four central multifunctional storage units, each composed from over five hundred uniquely formed wooden cubes. Curving playfully throughout the space, these units divide the 200-square-meter room into smaller areas accommodating the food lab, the herb garden, staff areas and an office. The raw, simple colors and forms help to capture a unique Nordic aesthetic. True to the restaurant's philosophy, the NOMA Lab is developed exclusively using Nordic materials. The organic forms of the furniture pieces stand out through use of integrated light features, which also lend the interior a lighter feel. This project presented an opportunity for GXN to experiment with digital design methods. They developed a form of living software, which made it possible to send drawings directly from the computer to fabrication. In practice, it meant that the interior was delivered as a three-dimensional puzzle of over 5,000 pieces that were assembled without the help of any carpenters.

↑ The structures of the former warehouse are still clearly visible in NOMA Lab.

↑↑ The freestanding work
desks allow plenty of room to
try and create.

↑ There are many different
ways to work in NOMA Lab.

↗ Ground floor plan
with kitchen, closet, office
and library.

→ In order not to endanger
the monument protection,
the shelves were built around
the existing building.

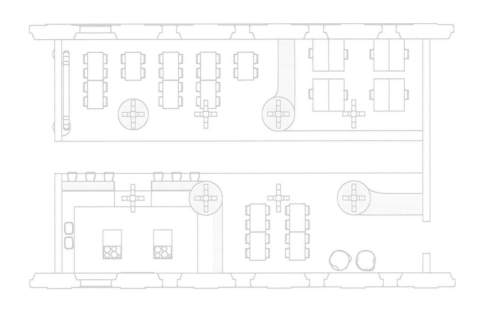

Château Faugères
Saint-Émilion, France

Architects → Mario Botta
GFA → 3,500 sqm
Completion → 2009
Client → Vignobles Silvio Denz
Inspired & inspiring → wine
Main materials → bearing structure in reinforced
concrete, cladding in Aragona stone
www.botta.ch

Atop the undulating hills near Saint-Émilion, in the Bordeaux area, swathes of vineyards stretch across the land—countless neat rows of vines rooted in the furrowed surfaces of the earth. In this landscape, the changes wrought by man are in perfect harmony with the metamorphoses of nature. It is here—in a region of poignant beauty suffused with history and memory—that Silvio Denz asked Mario Botta to design a new winery. Characterized by formal simplicity, the construction comprises a large stone building, part of which resides underground. The treading of the grapes takes place on the ground floor, while the areas for the production and the ageing of the wine are located on the underground levels. A tower, characterized by a regular pattern of openings, rises up in the center of the building. It houses the administrative services and a cozy space for wine tasting. At the top, a covered terrace oriented towards southeast overlooks the countryside. The external façade in natural yellow stone accentuates the geometric outline of the composition. The project sets rational architecture created by man against the organic transformation of the landscape, enhancing the beauty of both.

↑↑ The monumental winery is situated at the top of the plateau overlooking Château Faugères.

↑ The winery integrates harmoniously into the UNESCO World Heritage site of Saint-Émilion.

↑↑ To improve the quality of the wine at every stage of production is a never-ending quest.

↑ The production and the ageing of the wine take place on the underground levels.

→ Château Faugères occupies 37 hectares of homogeneous land with some of the finest terroirs in Saint-Émilion.

↗ Ground floor plan with wine barrels.

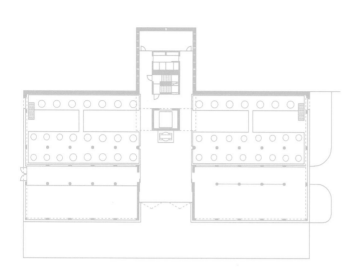

↑ To make wine is a labor of
love which requires time, hard
work and meticulous care.

House of Vans London
London, England

Architects → Tim Greatrex Architects/Hellicar Studio
Location → Arches 228–232 Waterloo Station Approach,
London SE1 7LY, England
GFA → 2,500 sqm
Completion → 2014
Client → Black Sparrow Presents/VF Corporation
Inspired & inspiring → art, food, video, music
Main materials → brick, rubber, concrete, wood
www.timgreatrex.com

The House of Vans London is a creative venue for Vans enthusiasts and those interested in skateboarding culture. It includes an art gallery, creative workshop spaces, a screening room, a live music venue, a café, numerous bars and an indoor concrete skate park. It sits within 150-year-old brick arches beneath the railway lines heading out of Waterloo station and next to a famous graffiti street. The area contains five individual tunnel spaces with a large rubber floor inspired by the iconic patterned sole of the Vans shoe. The site is delineated into four main activities: skateboarding, art, film and music. Used, re-appropriated forms and materials from skateboarding culture are utilized in the architectural installations. The design features many layers of different materials, from the existing raw brickwork tunnels to a clean color and texture palette. Outdoor metal halide flood lighting and neon lighting—both non-glare—illuminate the subterranean environment. Audio and video feeds can be streamed live from the venue, while the art gallery allows artists to display the work they produce in the Vans labs—a series of studio spaces. The kitchen has been designed not only for catering, but also to provide a space for food workshops. Screens in the café display live footage from the skate park.

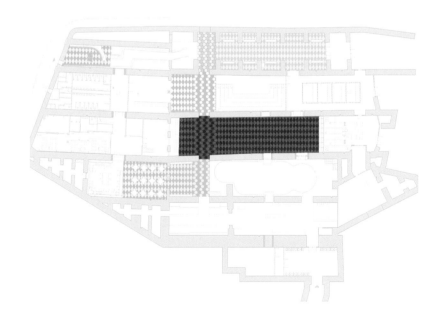

↑↑ The durable and recyclable rubber floor contrasts beautifully to the raw and textured brick walls and vaulted ceilings.

↑ Ground floor plan with the iconic patterned floor.

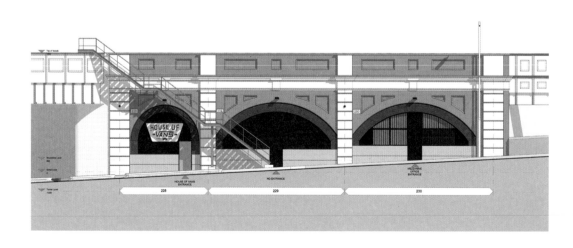

← Façade with 150-year-old brick arches.

↖ The bowl area for advanced and professional use is the central focus of the skate park.

↑↑ The House of Vans London includes a live music venue for 850 people.

↑ The branded signs in neon light create evocative focal points within the space.

"Let us together create the new building of the future, which will be everything in one form: architecture and sculpture and painting."

→ Walter Gropius

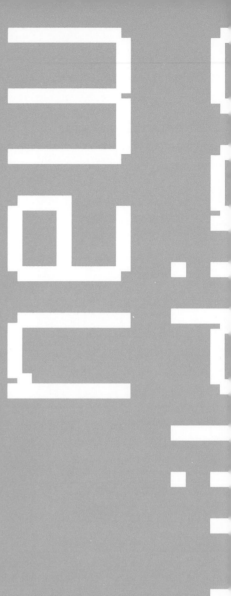

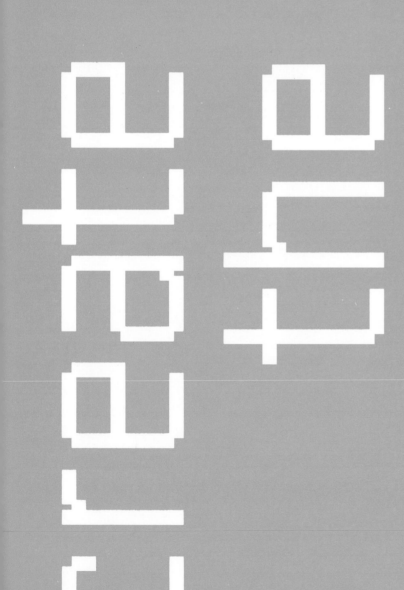

beginning of the future.

Ashton Old Baths
Tameside, England

Architects → MCAU
Location → Henry Square, Stamford Street West,
Ashton-under-Lyne, Tameside OL6 7TP, England
GFA → 650 sqm
Completion → 2017
Client → PlaceFirst Ltd / Tameside MBC
Inspired & inspiring → media, design
Main materials → plywood, Western Red Cedar,
double-glazed screens, dry-lined painted interior walls
www.mcau.co.uk

The new vision for the Grade II listed former municipal swimming baths was to bring the building back into use as a creative, digital and media hub. The project was split into two separate phases: Phase 1 included the complete restoration of the former main pool hall and the entire building's exterior, as well as the introduction of modern office space in the form of an independent freestanding structure. Phase 2 will see the future restoration and fit-out of the adjacent annex. The new self-contained, freestanding structure provides new workspace units with additional meeting rooms, break-out areas, and a new rooftop communal terrace. The exterior of the building has been completely restored and refurbished to preserve the Victorian heritage of the structure. The organic form not only helps to exploit borrowed daylight from the existing high-level windows, but also maintains the impact of the former pool hall's large open space and allows the existing building's internal fabric to remain visible. By providing new floor levels throughout, the overall visitor experience has been enhanced and different parts of the existing building can be appreciated in much closer proximity and from vantage points never previously realized. The synergy between the new intervention and the historic fabric creates a truly unique environment, designed to inspire and engage its visitors. This is particularly apparent when standing in the sensational event space located on the top floor, where the visitor is within touching distance of the beautifully crafted hammer beam roof.

↑ The new timber
structure contrasts with the
original inner fabric.

↑↑ An external view
from Henry Square.

↑ The new offices are
located in the middle of the
former pool.

↗ The ground floor plan
with the former pool and the
new timber structure.

→ The office space
at Level 0 also shows the
old structures.

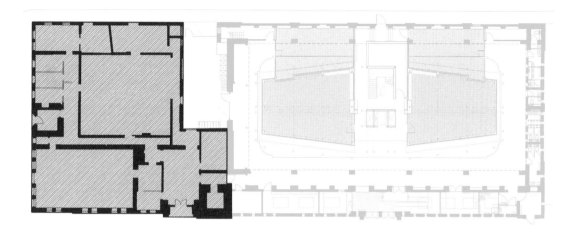

West Elm Maker's Studio
Brooklyn, NY, USA

Architects → VM Architecture & Design
GFA → 1,078 sqm
Completion → 2016
Client → West Elm
Inspired & inspiring → design
Main materials → concrete, wood steel
www.vmdstudio.com

West Elm's brand leadership and creative teams asked VMAD to design an off-site lab where they could bring together their product designers and creative teams to work in a hands-on, artistic environment. They wanted their teams to get away from their computers and desks and get back to their craft. The result is West Elm's new Maker's Studio. VMAD created a state-of-the-art complex within a historic warehouse located in Sunset Park, Brooklyn. The space was designed to facilitate interactions between West Elm's design and development teams, providing individual spaces, tools and equipment, as well as collaboration space. The various workshops covered all the creative business channels of West Elm including a ceramic studio, a weaving and textiles studio, a fully equipped woodworking shop, a metal working studio, a wood finishing lab, and a textile dyeing and color studio. Each space is fully loaded with modern equipment and features, including two kilns, pottery wheels, hoods and spray booths for the ceramics studio, various types and sizes of looms, paints, paper and brushes for the arts and crafts room, and a Makerbot 3-D printing room. Each studio was custom-designed to the programming requirements provided by the team. Large communal spaces under the skylights allow for the various teams to interact, exchange ideas and share their current projects.

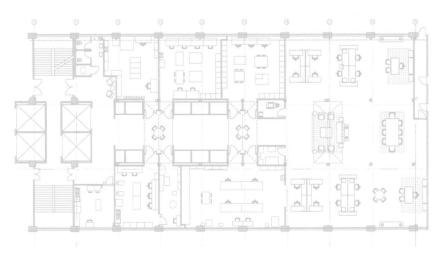

← In the painter's studio, the
art pieces are made by hand.

↑ West Elm Maker's floor plan.

↑↑ The craft room
offers plenty of space and
light for creative work.

↗ The workshops are fully loaded with equipment needed for the creative users.

→ The West Elm Maker's Studio is stocked with raw materials.

Holzschnitzerei Perathoner
Lajen, Italy

Architects → bergmeisterwolf Architekten
Location → Pontives 32, 39040 Lajen, Italy
Completion → 2012
Client → Ulrich Perathoner
Inspired & inspiring → carved wooden sculptures
Main materials → wood, glass
www.bergmeisterwolf.it

This new build was designed to evoke the long tradition of Grödner handicraft and the wood on which it depends. The process of manipulating wood is at the heart of the design. The façade features the same visual and textural irregularities found in wood, presenting itself as a vast wooden sculpture. This impression is strengthened by the irregular ageing of the shingle. The self-supporting folding system composed of triangles, accentuated by the surrounding gutter as a shadow gap, can also be sensed and experienced in the interior. There is just one section of steel framework in this pure wood structure; at this juncture, the façade is fully glazed to enable the greatest possible amount of light to enter the exhibition space. The outer walls comprise a number of triangular, reinforcing elements, each with two different gradients. From an architectural perspective, the façade provides a stable surface structure, but one that cannot bear huge vertical loads. Because of this, the load-bearing elements in the interior were designed to be stronger. Reinforced concrete was used for the stairwell core with goods elevator. The ground floor was designed to be almost devoid of interior walls, while on the upper level the various partition walls function as load-bearing elements of different thicknesses. A large exhibition space was created on the bottom level and extends over two stories. Workshops and storage rooms are found on both the upper and lower floors. On the roof level, the façade becomes part of the balustrade, enabling the creation of a sheltered space with roof terrace.

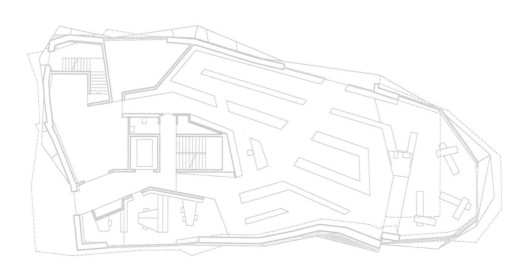

↑↑ Due to the wooden
cladding of the building, it fits
in well with the landscape.

↑ Ground floor plan.

← The unusual shape of the building itself looks like carved.

↑↑ Due to the many nestings of the building, light falls in several places in the room.

↑ The light that comes through the large glass windows is important for a detailed work.

↑↑ Glass and wood— the two main components of the construction.

P Blok Production Studio
Istanbul, Turkey

Architects → Iglo Architects
Location → Dereboyu Cad. G-41 Sok. 8/2
34485 Maslak, Istanbul, Turkey
GFA → 450 sqm
Completion → 2010
Client → P Blok / Utopia Fotograf Produksiyon
Inspired & inspiring → photography
Main materials → steel, glass, gypsum panels,
epoxy, wood, sandwich panels
www.iglo.com.tr

This project involved the transformation of a 450-square-meter warehouse in Maslak into a photography and production studio along with office and café functions. The aim was to create a spacious and attractive interior, while remaining within a limited budget. A series of contrasts structure the design—permeable and isolated spaces, light and dark, black and white—while the functional scheme between the offices, postproduction and studio areas and the supportive spaces such as café, makeup room, storage room and toilet facilities is solved optimally at the horizontal and vertical planes. Gray and transparent (glass) surfaces and warm woods in the furniture and upper story flooring break up the potential monotony of the largely black and white color scheme. The only change to the existing façade was a new coat of paint, while a ramp and rolling shutter at the entrance were retained as a useful means of bringing photography equipment for large-scale projects into the building. A new entrance door was added for the new reception area to the right. Two additional stories were also added on this side for the offices and postproduction units. At the rear, the full eight-meter ceiling height is used for the creation of the two studios. During the construction phase of the project, the neighboring office (belonging to the same landlord) was being moved and the structural steel elements were removed and reused in P Blok, serving the project's goal of economic sustainability.

→ View from the hallway
to one of the photography
studio areas.

↑↑ The offices and meeting spaces in the second story are glass-walled.

↑ A rustic staircase leads from floor to floor.

→ The studio is not only specialized in photography, but also in all kinds of production and postproduction needs.

↗ Ground floor plan with both photography and production areas.

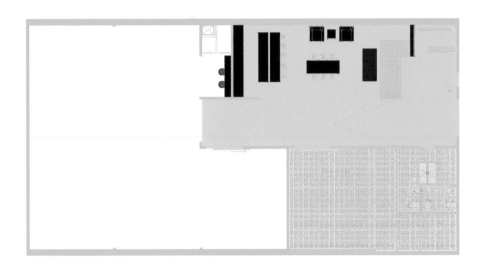

Toormix Workshop
Barcelona, Spain

Architects → Vora
GFA → 18 sqm
Completion → 2012
Client → Toormix
Inspired & inspiring → graphic design
Main materials → wood
www.vora.cat

Toormix Workshop is housed in a very small ground floor space (a former shop) facing the street. All surfaces are paneled with plasterboard and the original floor is covered with phenolic parquet. The architects were asked to design a multipurpose room for a team of graphic designers that could be used as a workshop or a showroom. For its regular use, it was necessary to define two environments: a working area with a large table and an informal relaxation and reading area. This was partly achieved by using different ceiling heights. But the two areas can also be merged for specific uses, such as for presentations or exhibitions. The relaxation area is defined by a wall cabinet, a door used as a support to exhibit magazines, and a corner with cushions and swings. Three large boards attached to the wall that can be unfolded to form three attached tables define the working area. Combinations of these boards in horizontal and vertical positions enable different forms of working and showcasing. Natural wood, white paint and blackboard are all incorporated into the boards, allowing for different uses. The opposite wall is partially coated with painted cork. A line of indirect lighting towards the ceiling illuminates the entire space, while a curtain rod covers the light armature and incorporates a guide for hanging paintings. This allows the wall to be used for temporary exhibitions. This low-cost refurbishment incorporates packaging plywood panels, raw walls and painted pavement in a realization that is closer to DIY than conventional architecture.

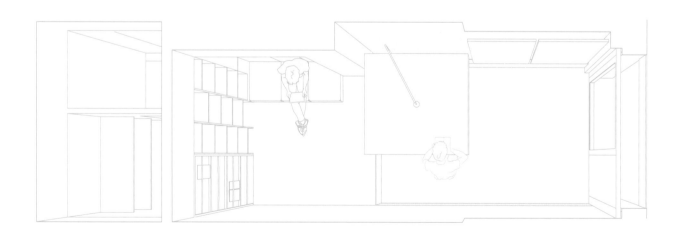

↑↑ The relaxation area can be used in different ways: swinging, reading or just relaxing.

↑ Stereoscopic view of the ground floor plan.

↑↑ View from a swing of the relaxation area in the minimalistic room of the graphic designers.

↑ In the working area, there are three large tables that can be folded individually.

→ The studio space is very small: only 18 square meters in a former shop.

Artist's Studio
Girona, Spain

Architects → Camps Felip Arquitecturia
GFA → 80 sqm
Completion → 2013
Client → confidential
Inspired & inspiring → art
Main materials → wood
www.arquitecturia.net

With the help of a carpenter, Camps Felip Arquitecturia built this 80-square-meter studio in the garden of an artist's house in just three weeks. To achieve this rapid construction, they used a pre-fabricated wood system that could be prepared in the workshop and then assembled on site. The L-shaped house generates a square garden dominated by a large ash tree. The plan of the studio is cross-shaped, where the main working space is double-height and the four wings accommodate the entrance, storage space, the sink and the living area. Everything is designed to be easily accessible. The volumes extruding from the center space feature large windows with views directed towards the outer corners of the gardens, giving the impression of maximum depth. A third window faces onto a paved driveway. Externally, everything has a pinewood finish in a warm tone that weathers well and harmonizes aesthetically with the garden. Pot plants are positioned on gray gravel under the windows in nooks created by the cross-shaped plan. These are intended to further integrate the building into the garden. The interior is lined in white-painted MDF boards with grooved surfaces. The high walls that surround the center of the space are used as a hanging area for paintings, while works in progress can be leant against the lower level walls. The double-height space provides breathing space for the artist and canvas, and gives a generous impression of light and openness.

↑↑ Pinewood finish
harmonizes perfectly with
its surroundings.

↑ The studio faces the
garden corners, so the artist's
house is not visible.

↑ The colorful artworks stand
out in the white room.

↑↑ The ground floor plan of
the studio is cross-shaped.

← The big tree in the garden fits in nicely with the many plants around the studio.

↑ The building is open and easily accessible.

passion. creating
s. creating

"I think space, architectural space, is my thing. It's not about façade, elevation, making image, making money. My passion is creating space."

→ Peter Zumthor

Ice House Court Studios
London, England

Architects → Delvendahl Martin Architects
Location → 56 Abbey Road, Barking,
London IG11 7BT, England
GFA → 470 sqm
Completion → 2016
Client → Bow Arts Trust
Inspired & inspiring → art
Main materials → timber, concrete, glass
www.dm-architects.co.uk

The creation of studio spaces for up to 25 artists in a new mixed-use neighborhood in Barking involved the fit out of an existing shell and core commercial space on the ground floor of a residential block. The site required a design response that balances the desire for public interface and interaction with the need for a degree of privacy associated with creative practice. Responding to the existing fully glazed façade, the primary intervention was a new timber screen and shelving system lining the perimeter of the spaces that provides a sense of continuity and rhythm throughout the studios, whilst simultaneously enabling the artists to embrace the shop front nature of the façade to display their work. In response to the limited project budget, the design relied entirely on standard and readily available components and materials. The color-stained timber profiles of the shelving system and white plywood panels also double up as a partitioning system, balancing a warm color palette against the raw concrete walls and floors. Bright yellow painted walls and floors demarcate the shared areas and highlight the two entrances in the otherwise homogenous elevation of standard glazing components. The project helps to retain artists in London with the Barking Artist Enterprise Zone delivering affordable, sustainable and flexible workspaces and homes for the benefit of the city's economy whilst also ensuring Barking's full potential is unlocked.

↑↑ Each artist can customize his studio individually and make it his own space.

↑ Detail of the ceiling and the timber shelving.

↑↑ Through a private
entrance, each room can be
entered from the street.

↑ The art contrasts sharply
with the raw concrete walls.

↗ Ground floor plan of the
Ice House Court Studios.

→ The studios are based in
the new Ice House Creative
Quarter in Barking, London.

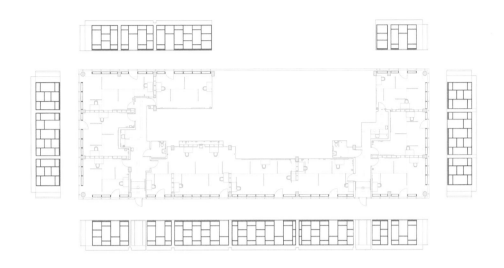

His & Hers Art Studio
Southampton, NY, USA

Architects → TBD Architecture & Design Studio
GFA → 55 sqm
Completion → 2009
Client → confidential
Inspired & inspiring → art
Main materials → cedar, polycarbonate
www.tbddesignstudio.com

The His & Hers Art Studio is designed for a couple and was built on the same site as their existing residence, nestled into a tree line at the edge of the property. The building is made up of two intersecting volumes: a steel frame with a translucent polycarbonate curtain wall and a wood frame with cedar siding and punched windows. The first volume houses a collage studio for Him and the second a ceramic studio for Her. In an effort not to damage any of the neighboring flora, the building shape was bent to fit between the existing trees and the foundation was designed to minimize disturbance to root systems. The elevated steel frame was designed such that when the concrete piers were hand-dug, should a large root be encountered, the pier could be relocated up to three feet away from their planned location and the root left intact. Distinctive skins on each volume reflect the two different working environments. The polycarbonate system creates a private and introverted space filled with diffused natural light while projecting colors and shadows from the surrounding environment onto the interior walls. The more typical wood-framed volume features a series of punctures, framing views of the yard and the house and generating a direct visual connection with the surroundings. From the main house, the studio can be seen from the entertaining areas and at night the translucent volume appears to glow or offer a light show directed by a spinning disco ball and a color changing spotlight.

↑ For the construction of the studio, nothing had to be removed from the environment.

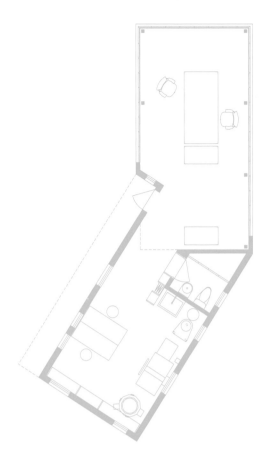

← View from the ceramic studio to the collage studio.

↑↑ The floor plan shows
the extraordinary shape
of the building.

↑ In addition to the lot of
light through the polycarbonate
wall, ceiling lightings brighten
up the studio.

↑↑ The collage studio
for Him.

Architekturladen
Marburg, Germany

Architects → Architekturladen
GFA → 60 sqm
Completion → 2010
Client → Matthias Schneider
Inspired & inspiring → architecture
Main materials → oak, aluminum
www.architekturladen.com

This project was inspired by the desire to integrate a modern architecture studio into the middle of Marburg's historic city center. The design should incorporate a combination of the new and the old, the modern and the traditional in a project that boldly represents contemporary life in the midst of the medieval. Wood—a classic material used as the sole building material for many centuries—is used as the primary substance, but in new and innovative ways. With its combination of oak, plastering and metal, the interior shows not only the interplay of old and new materials, but also makes legible how architecture has changed over time. During the renovation process, the main structure was exposed, gutted and cleaned and the floor plan reorganized. The result was a bright, sunlit and open creative space with wonderful views. The layout of the studio reflects the type of work that goes on here: lighting and illumination, architecture and interior design. The design of the interior is in full aesthetic harmony with the existing building structure. The floors are made of high-quality oak, while the existing girders were cleaned and left with their original surface texture. The walls and sloping roof are plastered in white, existing window openings were reconstructed, and the panoramic glass façade was given a fresh architectural inter-pretation. Parts of the ceiling were removed, while its supporting structure remained intact, generating new views and increasing the amount of sunlight entering the studio.

↑↑ During the conversion, a gallery was pulled into the office to allow breaks and a great view into the distance.

↑ The old town as inspiration for new creation.

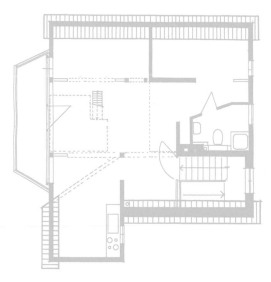

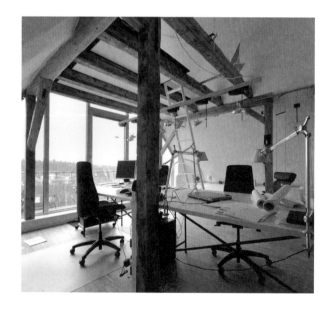

← Ground floor plan with office, kitchen, toilet, archive and gallery.

↖ The floor of the office is adapted to the originally installed material, oak.

↑↑ The glazed front not only allows a great view over the city, but also provides enough light to work.

↑ The rustic structure of the old building blends well with the simplicity of the modern interior.

Taller de Pintura
Los Vilos, Chile

Architects → Felipe Assadi Architects
Location → Condominio Bahia Azul Sitio 14,
Los Vilos, Coquimbo Region, Chile
GFA → 55.5 sqm
Completion → 2014
Client → confidential
Inspired & inspiring → art
Main materials → board-formed concrete
www.felipeassadi.com

This painter's studio is located on the edge of a cliff on the shore of the Pacific Ocean. It comprises a small board-formed concrete prism embedded in the slope, with at least a third of its length cantilevered towards the sea. It is located at the highest point of the site so that the roof of the studio is an extension of the garden that precedes it. Access is created by a cut in the hill and the roof was designed with wild plants around a wooden deck. The main structure consists of two longitudinal lines which have no perforations and act as two large beams embedded in the hill. One of them receives indirect sunlight that bathes the developing paintings below in diffused light. The other is a wall-program, which houses the necessary furniture for painting, the sink for the brushes, a storage area for paint, the fireplace, and even a complete bathroom inserted into a wall that protrudes toward the exterior of the concrete. The central space is situated between the two extremities of the studio: on one end the edge that faces the sea, and on the other a small interior garden near the entrance. A narrow metallic staircase, very transparent, has been developed over the excavated rock, leaving the user apart from everything. The project functions as a refuge from the surrounding constructions, the interior permeated only by indirect sunlight entering from above.

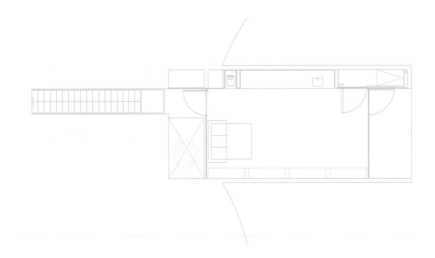

← The garden around the
building merges with the roof

← Ground floor plan of
the painting studio.

↖ The entire building is
constructed of board-formed
concrete, giving it a clean look.

↑↑ The large glass front
in the studio provides a great
view of the Pacific Ocean.

↑ Through its overgrown
roof and restrained design,
the studio fits perfectly into
the landscape.

Alex Monroe Workshop
London, England

Architects → DSDHA
Location → 42 Tower Bridge Road,
London SE1 4TR, England
GFA → 200 sqm
Completion → 2016
Client → Alex Monroe
Inspired & inspiring → jewelry
Main materials → corten steel façade,
birch plywood interiors (lining)
www.dsdha.co.uk

Located between a pub and a shop, this newly built four-story workshop presents an enigmatic and finely crafted storefront. Its bespoke weathered steel external skin responds to the eclectic surrounding brick architecture, whilst clearly signaling the building's function as being neither retail nor residential. The façade's horizontal metal blades establish a rhythmic harmony with the composition and articulation of the immediate streetscape, whilst achieving a moiré-like visual effect. This veiled appearance acts as a protective shield, allowing passers-by at ground level to catch a few glimpses of the activities inside. It is a form of architecture that is in conversation with its context, and with the people who inhabit the area. A generous "social" staircase is located at the entrance next to the workshop (just behind the street façade) connecting the different floors, activities and users visually and acoustically. On the first floor a roof terrace provides a verdant refuge for the artisans, away from the busy street and the work of jewelry making, and above the web and design studios with views back across the city. Light is constantly modulated and captured to reinforce a sense of connectivity with nature throughout the building. The aim was to create a convivial workspace capable of mediating between the interior sphere and the city, between making at a small scale and participating in wider world networks. In doing so the space preserves and nurtures creativity and the cultural infrastructure that enriches the city.

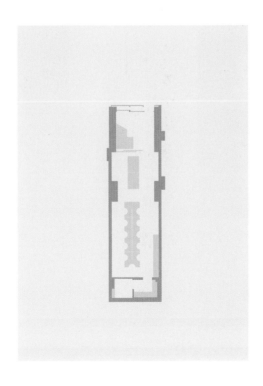

↑↑ The ground floor work-
shop where the jewelry is made.

↑ Ground floor plan with
entrance lobby, workshop,
WC and machine room.

↑ The "social" staircase leads through the building.

↑↑ The workshop on the ground floor has an open workspace.

↗ View up through the "social" staircase.

→ View from Tower Bridge Road—the workshop is located between a pub and a shop.

He, She & It
Buffalo, NY, USA

Architects → Davidson Rafailidis
GFA → 140 sqm
Completion → 2015
Client → confidential
Inspired & inspiring → art
Main materials → wood, metal, polycarbonate
www.davidsonrafailidis.net

This 140-square-meter new build contains workspaces for a painter
and a ceramist / silversmith, as well as a greenhouse. These three
uses are housed in three distinct buildings (He, She and It), merged
into a single structure. The spaces are grouped to form a cluster
of three mono-pitched sheds. At the surfaces where these sheds
connect, the walls are removed up to a height of around two meters.
The remaining ridge wall segments above act as structural trusses
to span the openings freely, making the structure appear to hover
over the open ground floor. While He, She and It appear as independent, materially distinct volumes—a white cube, a wooden shed
and a greenhouse—structurally and climatically they are also depen-
dent on one another. The unique atmospheres reflect not only the
current uses of each building, but also the inhabitants themselves who
are free to alter the function of their space. It is often visitors who
suggest new, unexpected scenarios, such as a summer bedroom
in the greenhouse. The climate conditioning strategy emphasizes the
intimate relationship that users have with the space, with each area
offering a different climatic barrier. Insulated interior sliding-folding
doors and exterior operable openings are used to adjust the space
to different weather conditions.

→ He, the white cube
with room to paint.

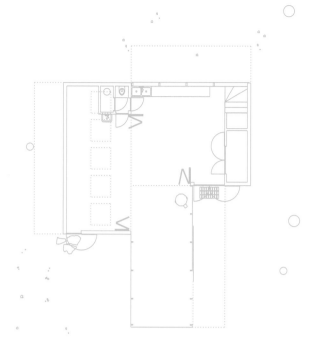

← It, the greenhouse
with its large translucent
polycarbonate surfaces.

↑↑ Ground floor plan in
warm weather.

↑ The different rooms all
merge into each other and thus
interact with each other.

↑↑ She, the wood shed,
overlooking the greenhouse.

Artist's Studio
Warsaw, Poland

Architects → Piotr Brzoza Architekten, Projekt Praga
GFA → 432 sqm
Completion → 2014
Client → Paweł Althamer
Inspired & inspiring → art
Main materials → steel structure, concrete blocks
www.brzoza.ch
www.projektpraga.pl

Paweł Althamer is one of the most renowned Polish contemporary artists for sculptures, performances, installations and video art. An ever-growing number of projects and exhibitions has forced him to expand his family atelier in Warsaw. His initial idea was to create a place where the family's two generations can work and spend time together, while preserving each person's independence. The development covers almost the whole area of the plot and groups it into various indoor and outdoor spaces, serving different users. There is also a central common space separate to the clearly assigned areas. Since the artist regularly invites visitors such as public officials, politicians, schoolchildren and disabled people to the space for communal artistic activities, it was crucial to develop a clear but not divisive gradation of privacy within the complex. The common courtyard is the most public space, followed by the atelier ground floor used for any kind of sculptural group work, then the mezzanine as a small meeting and office area, and finally a small, fully private and concealed room that can be entered through a small opening in the mezzanine wall. The last room is located within a geometrically deformed, golden object protruding from the main structure, just above the entrance to the central courtyard. The golden capsule serves as a place of seclusion and meditation for the artist and can be perceived as an architectural interpretation of Althamer's art, which is inspired by aerospace.

↑↑ In the large courtyard
private meets public.

↑ The open design makes it
possible to link work and family
life for the artist.

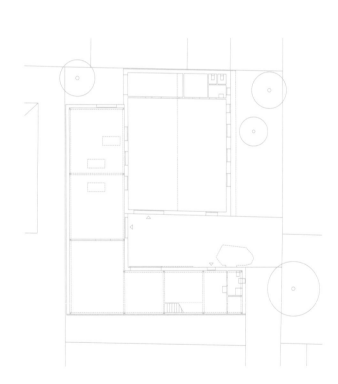

↑↑ Officials and politicians also come to the studio to participate in communal artistic activities.

↑ The floor plan shows the different areas of the studio, private and public ones.

↗ Through the transparent façade, the large areas of the studio can be seen.

→ In the golden capsule, there is a small room used by the artist for rest and relaxation.

"We do not create the work. I believe we, in fact, are discoverers."

→ Glenn Murcutt

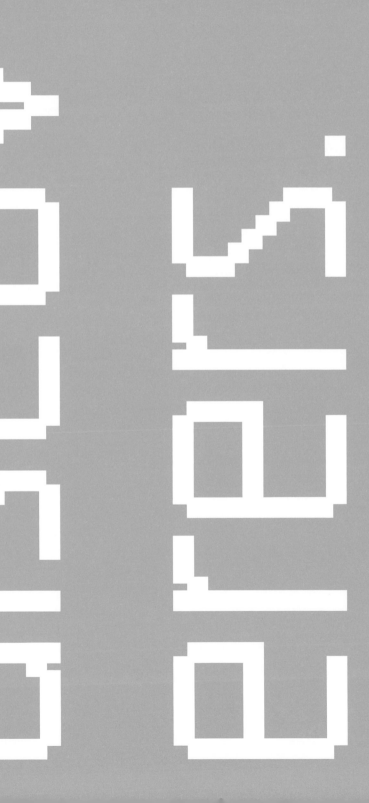

House and Atelier for an Artist
Gijón, Spain

Architects → Miba Architects
GFA → 398 sqm
Completion → 2013
Client → confidential
Inspired & inspiring → art
Main materials → steel, concrete
www.mibaarq.com

This house and studio are part of a larger research project looking at the integration of architecture and landscape at different scales. The proposed design was a hybrid of two typologies: the modern house and an industrial shed. Three autonomous but interrelated units—house, guest apartment, and atelier and garage—interact with the natural slope to enable the integration of the two types into a single volume. The structure emerges from the slope at one extreme and detaches itself on the west side. An open hallway located in the central area where the house and atelier merge is designed as both an exterior and a roofed space that draws the two typologies into dialogue and regulates the climate of each. The construction is based on a metal corrugated plate exposed in the interior, with a thermal layer of ten centimeters that covers the whole volume and an exterior finished in flexible stucco on fiber reinforced resins. The vertical walls are made of honeycomb clay block that reinforce the thermal insulation from the outside and increase the interior thermal lag. In the guest apartment, the thermal blanket is substituted with a garden roof that establishes continuity between the garden and the building and provides insulation.

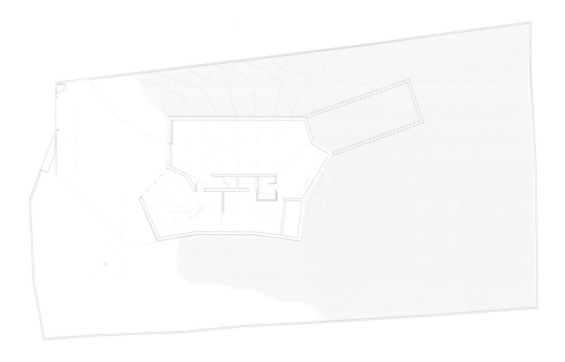

↑↑ Exterior view of
the building.

↑ Floor plan of the house with
the surrounding landscape.

← Through its simple and clear design, the studio focuses on the artworks.

↑↑ The large glass windows also let the kitchen merge with the surroundings.

↑ The lawn does not only lead around the house, but also covers it.

↑↑ The kitchen was kept very minimalist and clear.

Wade Davis Author Studio
Washington, D.C., USA

Architects → Travis Price Architects
GFA → 18 sqm
Completion → 2004
Client → Wade Davis
Inspired & inspiring → text
Main materials → stucco, wood, glass
www.travispricearchitects.com

The project was simple: 18 square meters generated by one tiny circular room off a small, refurbished greenhouse lined with books. A number of books have been crafted here, as well as debates and TED talks. The formative idea was to put the books that are most important to the Canadian anthropologist and author Wade Davis high up, as if they are floating above his head at all times. The dome shape above is a visual echo of an ancient Greek Tholos—the shape of a pregnant woman's belly. It represents the idea of intellectual birthing, a Socratic midwife bringing new ideas into the world. The wooden floor hub below is shaped as a circle, with a high-tech metal extension ladder extruding upwards, as if emerging out of a Kiva ceremony. A skylight connects the interior visually with the wider world via glimpses of the sky, while a horizontal slit window allows glimpses of the green garden. The exterior building shape is reminiscent of an ancient tree trunk. Back inside, the studio itself is home to countless mysterious items, including a blue-horned sheep skull from Mount Everest, Peruvian weavings, and native tapestries.

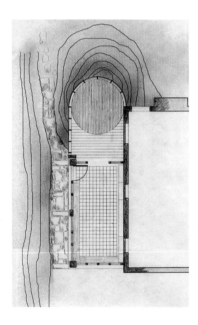

← The shrine, one foot in
the earth and birth in the
sky surrounded by the wolf's
eye and relics of time.

↑↑ Looking upward above
the Kiva at the Socratic Sky.

↑ Floor plan of the
restored greenhouse and
new Kiva Cave Circle.

→ Looking back at the hidden
procession of enlightened
books in the light-filled cave.

Lakewood Art Studio
Miami, FL, USA

Architects → KZ Architecture, Inc.
Location → 19720 NE 23rd Ave, Miami, FL 33180, USA
GFA → 430 sqm
Completion → 2011
Client → confidential
Inspired & inspiring → art
Main materials → metal, glass, concrete
www.kzarchitecture.com

An artist's studio addition to an existing home served as a catalyst
to transform a backyard into a series of terraced outdoor rooms,
pulling an indoor lifestyle out into the subtropical climate. Nestled
between mature oak specimens in the front and a lake in the rear,
the single-story vanilla box home lacked a connection to its subtropical setting, while the vast but decaying spaces in the rear of the
2,137-square-meter site were in desperate need of an intervention.
The clients approached the architects with the request to add
an art studio for the mother (a painter) on the northern edge of the
property. They also sought a re-design of the outdoor areas, which
comprised a worn-out fabric canopy, a pool and a large expanse of
unusable open space sloping down to the lake. The architects provided a well-lit studio with ample work and wall space as well as an
office and a bathroom. The outdoor space now features a covered
terrace and the so called "Bar-B-Q" area perfect for entertaining.

↑ The two tall concrete pillars
help separate the outdoor living
space from the pool area.

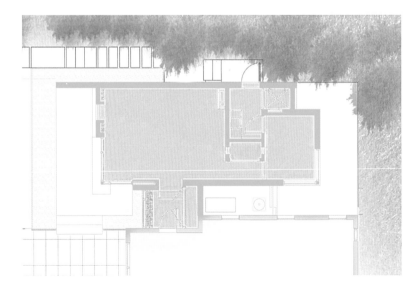

↑ Floor plan of the art studio adjacent to the house.

↑↑ Interior view of the art studio.

→ The studio addition seems to float above the home's new terracing.

↑ The upper canopies provide coverage for outdoor living and sunshades.

Anagram Office
New Delhi, India

Architects → Anagram Architects
GFA → 300 sqm
Completion → 2013
Client → Anagram Architects
Inspired & inspiring → architecture
Main materials → recycled wood,
stone veneer, micro concreting
www.anagramarchitects.com

Anagram's philosophy is reflected perfectly in the design of this new office. Much larger than the previous establishment, with long, broad tables and open-plan spacing, the office has an atmosphere that echoes the look and feel of a basic architectural studio from the past, despite the obvious presence of modern technology. The idea was to generate a space that invited discussion, debate and evolution. The innovative entrance staircase was envisioned as a broadly public zone, where employees could sit and unwind or interact with each other. Despite its basement location, the office is filled with natural, diffused light that enters via skylights and light wells skirting the external basement walls. A large mural of a mechanistic ant covers the back wall of one sky-lit gallery, flanking the visual expanse of the studio. Created by artist Anpu Varkey, Ant-1 was conceptualized as a reflection of the underground nature of the premises while drawing parallels with the characteristics of collective intelligence and shared work exemplified by the insect.

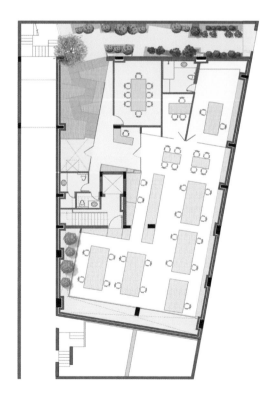

↑↑ In the entrance area,
the visitor is greeted directly by
the striking green staircase.

↗ The characteristic
staircase can also be seen
on the floor plan.

← Regardless of their actual function, the staircase can also be used as a breakout space.

↑↑ The giant ant on the office wall is a real eye-catcher.

↖ The offices are designed for an easy and creative communication between employees.

↑ The green color can be found everywhere in the office.

Brickfield Studios
London, England

Architects → Sarah Wigglesworth Architects
Location → Empson Street, London E3 3LU, England
GFA → 2,801 sqm
Completion → 2015
Client → Space Studios
Inspired & inspiring → art
Main materials → brickwork, blockwork, new glazing,
insulated roofing panels, galvanized steel shutters
www.swarch.co.uk

A former print factory has been fully refurbished to provide 50 studios over two floors. Brickfield Studios was a freehold purchase in 2014 and completed and let to artists in early 2015. Set in "the last patch of the old East End" it is located in an area of factories and garages. The project includes the conversion of the existing industrial building into art studios including the insertion of a new internal mezzanine and staircases creating new floor space and kitchen areas. The project also involves the alterations and adaptations required to the existing building in order to support this use. Two new light wells have been created around the staircases providing double-height spaces for communal use, meetings, exhibitions, loading bays and for artists to meet one another outside of the studio context. The new windows and the roof improve the building's overall thermal performance as well as providing better levels of natural light to the studios. A simple palette of blockwork infill is used to leave a trace of the former openings and to contrast with the brickwork of the existing building. Security shutters to the ground floor windows are simple boxy additions that are in keeping with the industrial context. A large roller shutter to the side of the building allows the studio space to open up to a covered loading bay for the construction of larger works or a place for social gatherings to take place. The original staircases and murals in the main office entrance are retained and have been refurbished, helping to tell the story of the building.

↑ Simple finishes to the rooms
allow the artwork to stand out.

↑ The large roller shutter opens the studio and space and makes it seem even bigger.

↑↑ The interiors of the studios are very simple and industrial, matching the building.

→ The old factory building offers enough space for all kinds of artistic activities.

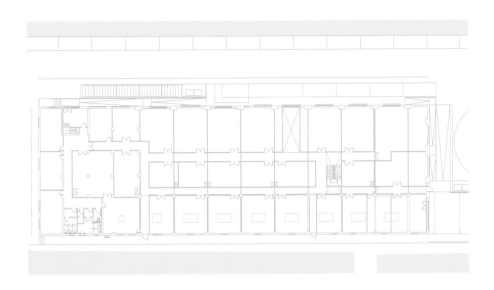

↑ Ground floor plan of
the former print factory with
the new studios inside.

Lune Croissanterie
Fitzroy, Australia

Architects → Studio Esteta
Location → 119 Rose Street, Fitzroy,
Victoria 3065, Australia
GFA → 420 sqm
Completion → 2015
Client → Lune Croissanterie
Inspired & Inspiring → pastries
Main materials → steel, concrete, glass
all within existing building shell
www.studioesteta.com.au

A small, hole-in-the-wall shop front used to be the home of Lune Croissanterie. Now it operates out of a large, old Fitzroy warehouse and has attracted international attention. The client sought a design that enabled fluid and seamless production whilst celebrating the products—the croissants and pastries—themselves. The solution was a division of the warehouse space into three distinct areas. The first area upon entering the space is dedicated to bakery service and consists of two monolithic concrete counters with ordering to the left and waiting to the right. This separation allows for customers to engage with the central illuminated and climate controlled glass cube, known as the Lune Lab. Dedicated to the production of the pastries, the cube is the heart of the operation. The third area to-wards the rear of the space is for baking and kitchen preparation. The design of Lune Croissanterie takes the rough and raw quality of the existing warehouse and retains and reinvigorates this with clean and minimalistic gestures, a considered and refined material palette, and clever spatial planning that allows for a seamless work and flow process for both the patrons and the staff. Aesthetics and functionality are addressed simultaneously to create a space that is both timeless and sustainable.

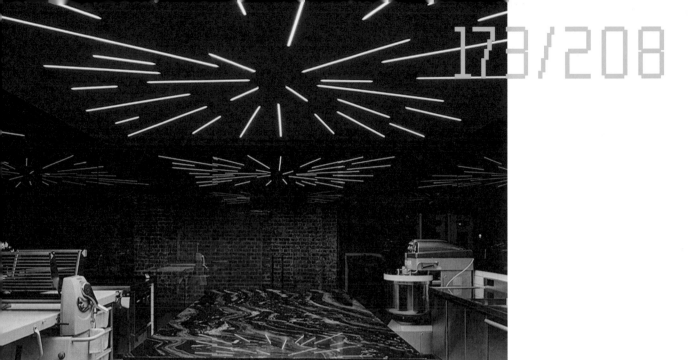

↑↑ The Lune Lab
blurs the boundary between
patron and baker.

↑ The glowing show space
glorifies the production
process enabling customers
to engage with the process.

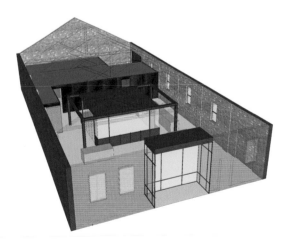

↑↑ The rough and raw quality of the existing warehouse was retained creating contrast against the transparent cube.

↑ 3-D rendering of the new parts in the old walls.

↗ Ground floor plan with the three areas including the Lune Lab.

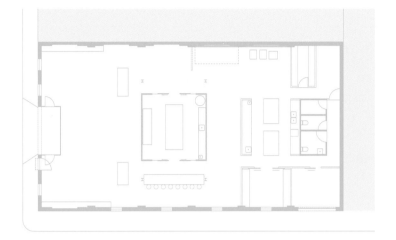

→ The new Lune Croissanterie operates out of a 400 sqm Fitzroy warehouse.

Anidan Children's Atelier
Lamu, Kenya

Architects → Urko Sánchez Architects
GFA → 108 sqm
Completion → 2013
Client → Anidan
Inspired & inspiring → art
Main materials → coral stone, mangrove poles, makuti
www.urkosanchez.com

Anidan is an NGDO founded by Rafael Selas Colorado to care for the needs of young children in Kenya. He houses over 140 children and feeds, dresses, cares for and educates around 250 in a shelter on the island of Lamu. Since 2008, there has also been a pediatric hospital. The children taken in by Anidan are the most vulnerable; they may be abandoned or orphaned, exposed to mistreatment or suffering from illnesses that cannot be cured in their current environment. The architect's work with Anidan began in 2007 when the assignment was to construct a shelter on Lamu Island housing around 200 children. The initial layout was for three buildings—separate dormitories for girls and boys, and an office, which also housed a kitchen and dining area. Local materials and natural ventilation were used, including huge makuti roofs to cool down the buildings and to generate open spaces via rooftop terraces for classes. The structures require low maintenance and are environmentally sound. The surrounding trees played a key role in determining the positioning of the structures. As the needs of the organization have increased, the architects were commissioned to design a hospital and an art workshop on the same plot. The new children's arts atelier required a multipurpose and ventilated space to house classes for drawing as well as sculpture, embroidery and other crafts. The result was a double space with storage and a cleaning area covered with a single makuti and surrounded with walls that are hung with pieces of art and installed at varying levels to shield the space from the wind.

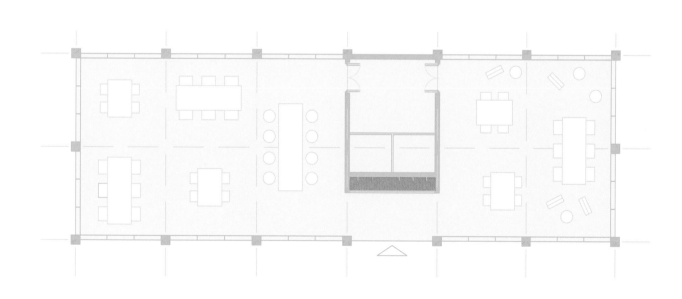

↑↑ The atelier is very
open and shows that
everyone is welcome.

↑ Ground floor plan
of the workshop.

⬉ The exterior of the Anidan
Children's Atelier in Kenya.

↑ In the atelier, there is plenty of room for the kids to come and be creative.

↑↑ The construction is adapted to the environment and kept very simple.

↑ The building also has a storage and cleaning area.

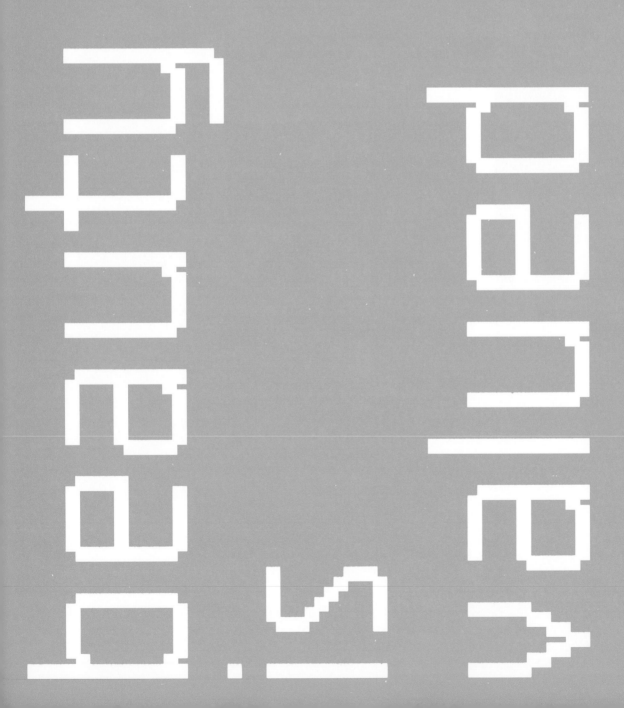

"For me beauty is valued more than anything—the beauty that is manifest in a curved line or in an act of creativity."

→ Oscar Niemeyer

more
than
anything

Büro
Munich, Germany

Architects → CBA Clemens Bachmann Architects
Location → Hans-Preißinger-Straße 8, building C,
81379 Munich, Germany
GFA → 242 sqm
Completion → 2017
Client → CBA Clemens Bachmann Architects
Inspired & inspiring → architecture
Main materials → black MDF, blockboard
www.cbarchitekten.com

The offices of CBA Clemens Bachmann Architects are located on a former industrial site with brick architecture to the south of Munich. Partial demolition exposed the basic framework of the old factory building and revealed the original dimensions of the space, which is flooded with natural light due to the high ceilings, the long south-facing window and the skylights in the sawtooth roof. A new zoning system was incorporated into the 220-square-meter space during the interior development phase. This involved the introduction of cubes with different functions, such as a kitchenette, a model-building space and an archive. These elements vary in height and volume and allow for a series of private meeting spaces, whose aesthetic—black and wooden—contrasts with the otherwise white, modest surroundings. The architecture of the space is in direct dialogue with the models created by those who work here: the workings and design of the interior and its installations remain prominent and visible. Presentation islands for models and materials frequently disrupt the clear workplace layout in dynamic ways. In its essence, this office space looks like an architectural workshop, in which different areas merge and various work processes complement and inspire each other. All of the current projects are made visible to the employees on presentation boards, inviting and stimulating discussion.

↑ Due to the sunlight that enters through the skylights and its generally bright design, the office looks luminous and open.

↑↑ The colors of the rooms are defined by the contrast between black and white.

↑ The office is not just a typical office but also a workshop for architectural models.

↗ The floorplan with spaces for office and workshop.

→ The lettering of the office units is also uniform and rich in contrast.

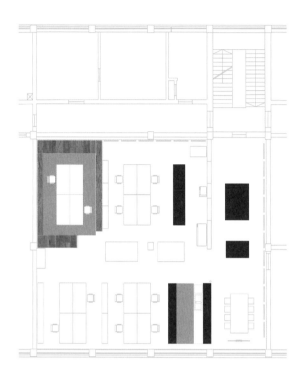

kitchen
storage
wardrobe

↑ In the meeting room, the employees are shielded from the rest of the workplace.

Painting Studio Nagoya
Nagoya, Japan

Architects → Ryohei Tanaka / G architects studio
GFA → 69.5 sqm
Completion → 2012
Client → private
Inspired & inspiring → art
Main materials → masking paint on concrete wall and ceiling
www.g-archi.info

Painting Studio Nagoya is the result of the renovation of a nondescript apartment room. The client was a painter, who bought the room in a 25-year-old apartment as a new habitat. His request was to create a small studio that doubles as a living room. Removing the wallpaper, the architect discovered old dirt and repair putty on the walls and concrete ceilings. For use as a studio, a rough finish seemed appropriate, but as a living room it was too dirty. The architect decided instead to make use of the unique texture, pasting resin sheet on the wall and painting it white. White paint was spray-painted on top of the stencil sheet, which was placed on the concrete surface. This procedure is the same as using a stencil graffiti template. The surface finish of the interior now incorporates both the original texture and fresh white paint. Reluctant to simply remove what was old, the architect chose instead to integrate the dirt, which tells the story of this apartment, into the new design. PVC sheet made of transparent resin—typically used as an anti-slip for furniture—was used for the stencil. The masking technique, often used in artistic paintings, was directly inspired by the client's profession as a painter.

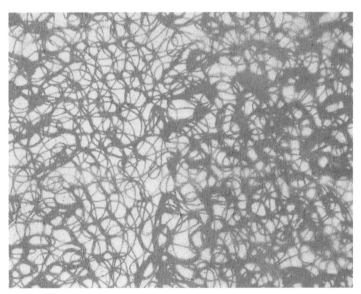

↑↑ The original texture of the building shows that behind the renovated studio is a building with history.

↑ Detail of the patterned wall.

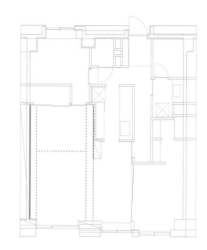

↑ The white color of the walls makes the studio look very bright.

↑↑ Ground floor plan of the apartment room which was renovated to a painting studio.

← The client, a painter, decided to make use of the old wall structure.

↑ Due to the minimalist furnishings, the peculiarity of the walls comes to the fore.

Garden Studio
Cambridge, England

Architects → Rodić Davidson Architects
GFA → 30 sqm
Completion → 2015
Client → Ben Davidson
Inspired & inspiring → architecture
Main materials → wood
www.rodicdavidson.co.uk

Hidden in amongst the trees at the end of a long garden, Rodić Davidson Architects have designed and built two separate timber-framed buildings for use as an office/studio and a model-making workshop. The structures are clad in vertical black-stained softwood boarding of varying widths—wider on the studio and narrower on the workshop. On the studio, the cladding forms a continuous rain screen that wraps the entire building. The larger studio building is highly insulated and incorporates a super-efficient air-source heat pump. In 2008 the architect/owner was offered some large Velfac glazed panels from a contractor who had ordered them mistakenly. For four years they sat in the garden under a blue tarpaulin. After his father's death in 2012, the architect inherited his grandfather's workbench and tools, which had been unused for almost 30 years. His grandfather was a carpenter by trade and was a major inspiration for the design, which was guided by the size of the workbench, the size and number of glass units, and the wish to not only store but also display the tools themselves. The workshop was built using a timber frame on a concrete base. The frame—set out precisely so as to form internal square sections—is clad with ply and then cross-battened and clad again with staggered roofing battens. Inside, peg-board was cut and placed between the stud work squares and the entire internal space was then prepared and sprayed with seven coats of Morrells satin lacquer.

↑ The grandfather's old
tools give the studio a special
ambience.

↑↑ In contrast to the façade, the interior is bright and illuminated.

↑ Bright wooden elements complete the design.

↗ Ground floor plan with both the office/studio and the model-making workshop.

→ The wooden buildings at the end of the garden stand out for their dark design.

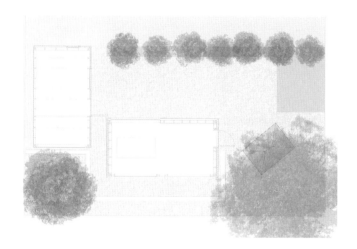

↑ The studios serve as
separate workplaces next to
the residential building.

Workshop House Tecnomec
São Paulo, Brazil

Architects → PAX.ARQ
Location → R. Amaro Cavalheiro, 85 – Pinheiros,
São Paulo – SP, Brazil
GFA → 385 sqm
Completion → 2015
Client → Tecnomec
Inspired & inspiring → mechanical engineering
Main materials → concrete, aluminum
www.pax.arq.br

As a result of particular programmatic requirements, this space was designed to host a residence and a mechanical workshop as well as classrooms. The programmatic activities were distributed so as to provide the greatest functional advantages for each. The result is a separation of the program into three levels: ground floor, which hosts the mechanical workshop activities, revisions, repairs, part-washing and a dynamometer room for vehicle testing; first floor, where the classrooms, study rooms and bathrooms are located; and second floor, the residence. All the activities are administered by a single inhabitant who divides his daily schedule between the different spaces, each characterized by specific elements. Perceived as a whole, each space interacts with the others in a unique and dynamic way. An inclined concrete slab with multiple functions plays a central role in the whole composition. It embodies the visual limit between the public and private realms, while sheltering the upper domains from noise pollution and the mechanical equipment on the ground floor. Simultaneously, it enhances natural ventilation and illumination for the workshop and classrooms, while facilitating the capture of rainwater for reuse. The relationship between the building and the surrounding urban environment is a compelling one, with the structure retreating from the terrain's limits and generating possibilities for gatherings and urban encounters.

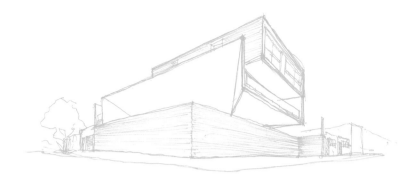

← The mechanical workshop is located on the ground floor and can be reached directly from the street.

↑ A single resident uses all facets of the building with its various areas.

↑↑ Sketch with the stacked areas.

→ From the workshop, the residence can be reached directly via a staircase.

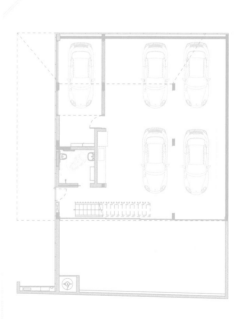

↑↑ The inclined concrete
slab makes it possible to accu-
mulate and reuse rainwater.

↑ Floor plan with cars in the
mechanical workshop.

Clarks Originals Design Studio
Somerset, England

Architects → Arro Studio
GFA → 300 sqm
Completion → 2015
Client → Clarks Originals
Inspired & inspiring → shoes
Main materials → solid wood, glass, steel
www.arro-studio.com

Located in a former warehouse, this project integrates several different zones into a harmonious whole. The space, part of the historical C&J Clarks site built in 1825, used to be the tools plant for the shoe manufacturer. The Arro Studio project splits the space into five different zones, each defining a specific function. An eight-meter-long floating table built around the existing INP beams creates a focal point for team members to gather and connect. The striking features of the surrounding historical buildings have been reinterpreted in a "modern factory," which is home to the director's office, a storage room and a large meeting room. The open workspace benefits from exceptional natural luminosity thanks to the large windows. Large cork panels, which can rotate and slide on the existing INP ceiling beams, help generate a versatile work environment that enables employees to open or close their own workspace, depending on their needs. A functional shoe wall at one end of the workspace functions as a giant closet. Each shelf, used to display the footwear designs, doubles up as handles that open to reveal a large amount of storage space. The leather storage area is made partly from translucent glass panels, which reveal the showcased leather rolls inside. The lounge area, located on the opposite side from the leather storage, integrates a small kitchen, a bar and a large storage bench system in the corner, as well as an oversized suspended light made out of metal welded tubes from which various leather hides are hanging.

↑↑ The walls of the historical
C&J Clarks site give the office
room a rustic look.

↑ Clarks' products are
displayed on a large shoe wall.

↑↑ Contrasting with the many wood in the office, the red design color stands out very much.

↑ The shelves are also made of wood and some are decorated with Clarks' own products.

↗ Ground floor plan with the different areas of the design studio.

→ The long wooden table forms the center of the office.

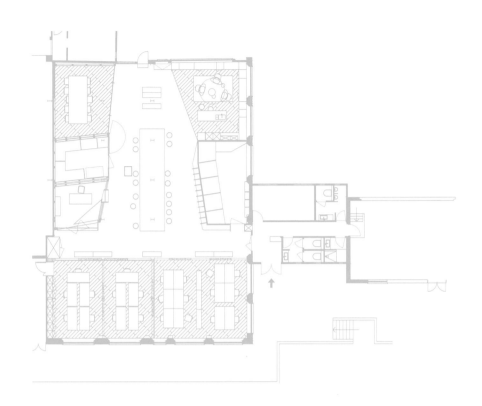

Park Street
Bristol, England

Architects → Holland Harvey Architects
Location → 85 Park Street, Bristol BS1 5PJ, England
GFA → 250 sqm
Completion → 2016
Client → Pinkmans Bakery
Inspired & inspiring → food
Main materials → copper, ebonized tulipwood
www.hollandharvey.com

This new concept restaurant and bar in a Grade II listed building
on Bristol's famous Park Street required extensive internal renovation
and a striking new storefront. The space features a copper-clad
counter, green wall and neon signage as counterpoints to the cool
palette of materials—the interior of the restaurant is designed
to respect the Victorian heritage of the site and create a warm and
welcoming environment in a popular and prominent location. Serving
pizza, cocktails and incorporating a full bakery, the design navigates
a complex brief through the use of clearly defined seating and dining
areas—providing café style to the front, and more formal seating
to the rear.

↑ Shop front with copper-
clad counter.

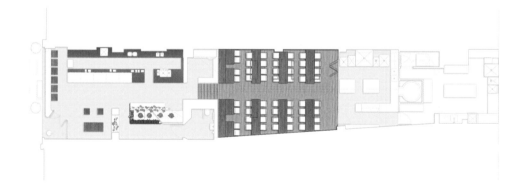

↑↑ Through the bespoke
screen, visitors can
watch the theater kitchen.

↑ Floor plan with
different areas.

→ In the theater kitchen,
food is prepared for the guests.

↗ The seating area with
bespoke lighting invites to
dine together.

Index

Picture Credits

Bharat Aggarwal 48–51
Fernando Alda, Sevilla, Spain 134–137
Arro Studio 198–201
Clemens Bachmann, Munich, Germany 183, 185
Gianni Basso 37–38, 39 b.
Jan Bitter 78–81
Tom Blachford 172–175
Boudewijn Bollmann, Rotterdam, The Netherlands 26–29
Tom Bonner, Los Angeles, CA, USA 40–43
Javier Callejas 176–179
Bruno Candiotto, São Paulo, Brazil 194–197
Enrico Cano, Como, Italy 86–89
Tim Crocker 123
Ben Davidson, London, England 190–193
Chris Dorley-Brown 168–171
Bernd Ducke, Ottobrunn, Germany 184
Ulrich Egger 105–106, 107 a. r.
André J. Fanthome 164–167
Francine Fleischer 53, 55
David Foessel 60–63
David Franck, Ostfildern, Germany 18–21
Takashi Fujino 30–33
Nathan Gallagher, London, England 90–93
Gareth Gardner, London, England 10–13
Adrià Goula, Barcelona, Spain 112–115
José Hevia, Barcelona, Spain 116–119, 152–155
Robin Hill, Miami, FL, USA 160–163
Oki Hiroyuki 22–25
Florian Holzherr, Gauting, Germany 142–145
Fethi Izan, Istanbul, Turkey 108–111
Adrian Lambert, Glossop, England 202–205
Beccy Lane, Manchester, England 96–99
Moreno Maggi 39 a.
Andy Matthews 14–17
Luca Miserocchi, Milan, Italy 138–141
Junten Morita 186–189
Adam Mørk 82–85
Nacasa & Partners 66–69
Sam Noonan, Adelaide, Australia 56–59
Dalton Portella 54
Maria Pujol Photographer 74–77
Agnese Sanvito, London, England 124–125
Matthias Schneider, Marburg, Germany 130–133
Scott & Scott Architects 70–73
Karolina Tunajek, Warsaw, Poland 146–149
Julian Wass, NY, USA 100–103
Günter Richard Wett 107 a. l., b.
Matthew Williams, New York City, NY, USA 126–129
Ken Wyner, Washington, D.C., USA 156–159
Shohei Yoshida 44–47

All other pictures were made available
by the architects and / or designers.

Cover front (from above to below): David Foessel, Karolina Tunajek,
Shohei Yoshida
Cover back: Takashi Fujino